And God Said...
Let There Be More
Laughter!

And God Said...

Let There Be More Laughter!

Humorous & Inspiring Stories, Quotes & Quips

Mary Hollingsworth

Guideposts
New York, New York

And God Said . . . Let There Be More Laughter!

Published by Guideposts
16 East 34th Street
New York, New York 10016
www.guideposts.com

Acknowledgments

Every attempt has been made to credit the sources of copyrighted material used in this book. If any such acknowledgment has been inadvertently omitted or miscredited, receipt of such information would be appreciated.

Scripture quotations marked (KJV) are taken from *The King James Version of the Bible.*

Scripture quotations marked (NCV) are taken from *The Holy Bible, New Century Version,* copyright © 1987, 1988, 1991 by Thomas Nelson, Inc. All rights reserved.

Scripture quotations marked (NIV) are taken from *The Holy Bible, New International Version.* Copyright © 1973, 1978, 1984 International Bible Society. Used by permission of Zondervan Bible Publishers.

Published in association with Mark Sweeney & Associates, Bonita Springs, Florida 34135.

Editorial, research, and content development managed by Creative Enterprises Ltd., Bedford, Texas. www.CreativeEnterprisesLtd.com. Team members: Rhonda Hogan, Mary Hollingsworth, Kathryn Murray and Barbara Tork.

Cover and interior design by Marisa Jackson
Typeset by Nancy Tardi

Printed and bound in the United States of America

With love and joy
to my mom,
Thelma Shrode,
who showed us how to laugh at life
even when times were tough.
Thanks, Mom!

Contents

Acknowledgments

This year marks my twenty-fifth anniversary working in publishing full-time. And what a ride it has been! One of the great lessons I've learned through these years is that you can't publish a book alone. If you try, you will be miserably disappointed in the results.

And God Said . . . Let There Be More Laughter! is no exception to that rule. Only with the help of a team of editorial and publishing experts is this book presented to you for enjoyable reading and encouragement. That experienced and professional team includes the following people to whom I owe my great appreciation and gratitude.

To God, Who created laughter and, thus, the opportunity for us to compile this upbeat and happy book.

To Guideposts Books, Linda Cunningham, and especially David Morris, who allowed us to participate in the production of this delightful product and encouraged us along the way. Thank you for giving us this great privilege.

To the entire editorial and production team, who have contributed to the development of this book: Patty Crowley, Vicki Graham, Rhonda Hogan, Sue Ann Jones, Laura Kendall, Mary Kay Knox, Kathryn Murray, Nancy Norris, Stephanie Terry and Barbara Tork.

Thank you, friends. You're the best!

Introduction

*A*nd God Said . . . *Let There Be More Laughter!* is the second compilation of stories, quips, quotes, and other funny bits and pieces created to delight and enlighten your days. We at Guideposts assembled a team to look high and low for funny and wholesome writings that celebrate the lighter side of living. This book and its predecessor, *And God Said . . . Let There Be Laughter!* are the result of that research. And we hope you have as much fun reading it as we did putting it together.

You'll find stories relating hilarious, real-life tales; rib-tickling jokes and cartoons; absurd, frozen-moment-in-time anecdotes; top-ten lists and other miscellaneous grin-getters; great quotations that make you smile; and some of the best one-liners we've ever seen.

The Bible doesn't actually record God as saying, "Let there be laughter," but He must have said it, winked His eye or nodded His head to bring it into existence because we have it. And oh, what a blessing it is! Without laughter, how would we survive the struggles and stresses of daily living? How would we face stormy days and scary nights? How would we live past the bumps and blasts on the road from here to heaven?

You can doubt it if you wish, but for us it's a no-brainer. In the midst of Creation, God definitely said, "Let there be laughter!" And after seeing its wonderful results on His people, with a big smile He reaffirms His intent by saying, "Let there be *more* laughter!"

Then we were filled with laughter,
and we sang happy songs. . . .

PSALM 126:2 (NCV)

1

Happily Ever Laughter

Marriage is like a roller coaster ride—one minute you're up and the next you're down. It's fun, exhilarating and terrifying. It's the ride of your life! A real white-knuckle event . . . filled with joy and commitment.

"YOU'RE MY BEST FRIEND IN THE WHOLE WORLD"

For a middle-aged mother of four, this is an adventure. I'm on a plane that just took off from Dallas-Ft. Worth, heading to a remote island in the Caribbean. Scott is beside me dressed in khaki shorts, a Hawaiian shirt and Teva sandals, topped off with an Aussie Outback-style leather hat. Oh, and he also brought his fishing pole aboard. Typical of my husband, he is fully *into* anything smacking of outdoorsmen thrills: lock, stock, and rod and reel. He's intensely absorbed in an issue of *Dive* magazine, occasionally stopping to show me a picture of tropical fishies, excited as a boy let out of school. He plans to become Scott Cousteau by week's end, I can tell.

I'm seeing glimpses again of the boy I fell in love with when I was a young girl of fifteen. After nearly a quarter century of babies, teens, bills and jobs, it's easy to forget that my husband is not just a father to our kids and payer of bills, but also my very best friend.

Our marriage needs a chance to remember that again. How long has it been since we embarked on a getaway— spent a few days just playing together?

We are en route to a small island in the Caymans because a kind-hearted, soft-spoken woman named Mary Brandis, whose family owns much of the property on Cayman Brac and Little Cayman, asked me to speak at a women's retreat. (She's calling it *Barefoot and Breaking Free* and is putting on this event as a gift to herself and to her friends, after what has been a very tough year.) She's ready to run free in the sand again, abandon herself to her Lord anew. Mary has invited between fifty and seventy-five American women and the same number of islanders to the Brac Reef Resort she owns and manages.

Scott, usually reluctant to accompany me to "ladies' things," took no time in offering himself as companion and bag carrier to "sacrifice for Jesus in the Caymans."

Yesterday, Mary called me at home from the resort as I was frantically searching for birth certificates to get Scott and me safely across the border. "I've found Scott's,"

I told her, "but mine seems to be missing. But, hey, here's a marriage license—I'll toss that in just in case I can piggy-back on his birth certificate by virtue of being legally married to him."

"Why don't you just keep looking for that birth certificate," Mary said with a laugh.

Minutes later, I hung up the phone and—*voila!*—found my birth certificate. Now we could prove I had been born, without having to drag my mother to the airport and make her show them her stretch marks. *Relief.*

But a funny thing happened today as we stood at the airline counter to purchase our tickets. "May I see your birth certificates?" the attendant asked.

"Sure," I said handing her the documents.

"Pardon me," she countered, directing her comments to Scott. "But this birth certificate does not match your driver's license. It says, 'Ezekiel Scott Freeman.' Are you Ezekiel?"

"No," Scott said, panic showing in his bulging eyes. "That would be my son." Then he turned to me. "Honeeeey, didn't you say not to worry, that you had my birth certificate?" I knew he was contemplating the scenario of his being left behind on a 105-degree August day in Texas, waving to me as I took off—alone—for cool island breezes.

I looked at the lady helplessly. "I must have accidentally grabbed my son's birth certificate instead of my husband's." With palms up, I shrugged toward Scott, who was now holding his head in his hands, and cheerfully added, "Whoops." It did not help.

A young man approached the counter to try to help. "Do you, by any chance, have your marriage license with you?" he asked.

Scott rolled his eyes and started to say, "Fat chance . . ." as I produced the needed document with the flourish of a magician. Indeed, he looked at me as if I'd just pulled a live rabbit out of my totebag.

> Since I enjoy staying a bit of a mystery to my husband, the only explanation I offered was a wide grin.

Since I enjoy staying a bit of a mystery to my husband, the only explanation I offered was a wide grin.

We've all heard jokes about "island time," so perhaps Scott and I should not be surprised that the pilot just announced—midair—that our connecting flight from Grand Cayman to Cayman Brac will be a bit delayed; he estimates about a four-hour wait.

I look at Scott and point to the Cayman Air insignia on the leaflet in front of us. "Well, what can we expect from an airline whose symbol is a peg-leg turtle?"

He laughs and we snuggle like sleepy kids, my head on his lap, as we wait for the landing, and the next plane that will take us to Paradise.

Becky Freeman

Marriage is like twirling a baton,
turning handsprings,
or eating with chopsticks.
It looks easy until you try it.

Helen Rowland

Two can live as cheaply as one . . . but only half as long.

Author Unknown

Four-year-old Suzie had just been told the story of Snow White for the first time in her life. She could hardly wait to get home from nursery school to tell her mommy. With wide-eyed excitement, she retold the fairy tale to her mother that afternoon. After relating how Prince Charming had arrived on his beautiful white horse and kissed Snow White back to life, Suzie asked loudly:

"And do you know what happened then?"

"Yes," said her mom, "they lived happily ever after."

"No," responded Suzie with a frown, "they got married."

Cecil Osborne

I know love is blind, but does it have to be deaf and dumb too?

Mary Hollingsworth

The best man was missing. The Baptist minister allowed them to hold up the wedding a few minutes waiting for him but soon resumed the ceremony routine.

When he asked for the ring, the errant best man popped up from the baptismal pool, snorkel and all.

Water dripped and his flippers flapped across the chancel floor as he unzipped his wet suit and handed over the ring.

Margaret G. Bigger

HUSBANDS

A husband shopping center was opened, where a woman could choose a husband from a wide selection of men.

It was laid out on five floors, with the men increasing in positive attributes as you ascended the floors. The only rules were that once you opened the door to any floor, you had to choose a man from that floor. And if you went up a floor, you couldn't go back down, except to leave the place.

So, a couple of girlfriends go to the shopping center to find a husband.

First floor: The door has a sign saying, "These men have jobs and love kids." The women read the sign and say, "Well, that's better than not having jobs or not loving kids, but let's see what's further up."

And up they go.

Second floor: "These men have high-paying jobs, love kids and are extremely good looking." "*Hmm*," say the girls. "But, what's further up?"

Third floor: "These men have high-paying jobs, are extremely good looking, love kids, and help with the housework." "Wow!" say the women. "Very tempting, but there's more further up!"

And so again, up they go.

Fourth floor: "These men have high-paying jobs, love kids, are extremely good looking, help with the housework, and have a strong romantic streak."

"Oh wow!" they exclaim. "But, just think what must be awaiting us further on!"

So, up to the fifth floor they go. The sign on the door says: "This is just to prove that women are impossible to please. Thank you for shopping, and have a nice day."

J. John and Mark Stibbe

I have some good friends who have been married many years. The wife calls the husband "Me." Out of curiosity one day, I asked her why. She said, "We are one flesh, which means I am him, and he is me. So I call him 'Me' as a constant reminder that he is part of me, and therefore I love him as much as I do myself."

That's some pretty good thinking!

Mary Hollingsworth

Then there was the guy who loved his wife so much, he almost told her.

Author Unknown

PULLING STRINGS

I'm married to a mellow fellow. It's a good thing because I don't think our house could take two of me. I'm so tightly strung, I need the balance of someone who has his feet on the ground.

I can identify with my friend Cindy, who said her husband, Craig, is like a balloon-man. He has both feet securely planted.

She's like a hot-air balloon, flying off in different directions. Craig watches her until she gets a little too far out, and then he takes hold of the string and pulls Cindy back down to earth.

Even though I'm grateful Les is a mild-mannered man, at times I wish he would show a little more enthusiasm. Recently I purchased a new dress, and I brought it out on a hanger for Les's viewing.

"What do you think?" I prompted.

"That's nice."

"Nice?" I cried.

"Didn't you ask me what I thought of your dress?" he asked, puzzled. "Your dress is nice."

"Les, 'nice' makes me nauseous."

"What do you want from me?"

"I want dramatic; I want dynamic; I want some enthusiasm!" I demanded loudly.

"Patsy, that dress is nice," he said with quiet firmness.

So I took the "nice" dress and stomped back to the closet.

On my way across the room, Les called out, "Patsy, look! Patsy, look!"

I turned and saw my two-hundred-pound husband leaping in the air, arms stretched heavenward, exclaiming, "Wow, what a dress! Wow, what a dress!"

I burst out laughing. My steady, ground-level man was behaving like a helium balloon.

Ever notice when we try to remake a person that we are seldom satisfied with the result?

Patsy Clairmont

**"If I die first, I'd like you to get married again.
But only if she's ugly, older than me, and no fun."**

THE RULES

1. The female always makes the rules.

2. The rules are subject to change without notice.

3. No male can possibly know all the rules.

4. If the female suspects the male knows all the rules, she must immediately change some of the rules.

5. The female is never wrong.

6. If it appears the female is wrong, it is because of a flagrant misunderstanding caused by something the male did or said wrong.

7. If the last rule applies, the male must apologize immediately for causing the misunderstanding.

8. The female can change her mind at any time.

9. The male must never change his mind without the express written consent of the female.

10. The female has every right to be angry or upset at any time.

11. The male must remain calm at all times, unless the female wants him to be angry or upset.

12. The female must, under no circumstances, let the male know whether she wants him to be angry or upset.

13. The male is expected to read the mind of the female at all times.

14. At all times, what is important is what the female meant, not what she said.

15. If the male doesn't abide by the rules, it is because he can't take the heat.

16. If the female has PMS, all the rules are null and void and the male must cater to her every whim.

17. Any attempt to document the rules could result in bodily harm.

18. If the male, at any time, believes he is right, he must refer to rule five.

Killy John and Alie Stibbe

GETTIN' THAR

Hiram had walked four long miles over the Great Smoky Mountains to court his lifelong sweetheart, Mary. They sat quietly for a long time on a bench beside Mary's log cabin. But soon that old devil moon worked its magic, and Hiram slid closer to Mary.

He patted her hand and said, "Mary, y'know I got a clearin' over thar and a team an' a wagon an' some hawgs an' cows, an I'low to build me a house this fall an' . . ."

Mary's mother, who had just awakened, interrupted Hiram at this point. "Mary," she called in a loud voice, "is that young man thar yit?"

Mary responded with a giggle. "No, Maw, but he's gettin' thar."

Cappers Weekly

My wife sure is immature. Every time I take a bath, she comes in and sinks my boats.

Tal D. Bonham

An old New England gentleman and his wife wanted to take a ride in a private plane, but they said the ten dollar charge was too much. The pilot offered them a deal. He would take them for a free ride if they promised not to say a single word during the trip. If they spoke, they would have to pay the ten dollars.

The trip passed without a word spoken. Back on the ground, the pilot said he hadn't thought they could do it.

"Well," the old man replied, "you almost won—I sure felt like hollerin' when Mama fell out."

Ralph L. Woods

PIECE OF CAKE

I checked the kitchen clock. Bill was due home any minute. Again, I would sit across the dinner table from him silently. As in silent treatment. At least, I hoped I would be silent. I was about ready to blow my stack. Tomorrow was my husband's final law exam. I figured it was cause to celebrate. So did he. But a three-day golf trip with his law school buddies? I pulled the casserole out of the oven and kicked the door shut harder than it needed to be kicked. My job paid his tuition. I put a square meal on the table every night. Dessert too. Didn't he want to celebrate with me? For the first time in eight months of marriage, I wanted to strangle him.

Mom warned me that sooner or later our lovey-dovey newlywed world would be rocked; we'd have our first fight. "Every couple does," she said. "Remember, it's not the end of the world, even if it feels that way." But I wanted Bill and me to stay in love forever, not fall into the rut of arguing like some old married couple. Since Bill had announced his golf plans, I'd held my tongue but cooked and cleaned with a vengeance: stripped the wax off the kitchen floor, reorganized closets, scoured the bathroom. Still, I couldn't cleanse myself of the resentment in my heart. Didn't Bill know how hurt I'd be? I don't think he even realizes I'm upset!

I ripped apart a head of lettuce. My eyes fell on the wedding picture I kept on the fridge. Bill and me, his hand over mine, as the camera caught us just about to slice into our triple-tiered cake. I'd wanted time to stop right then and there, our future full of hope as pure and sweet and untouched as the perfect white confection at our fingertips. Part of me hated to push the knife into the icing.

The icing! I hadn't iced the yellow box cake I'd made for tonight's dessert. That man has me so mad I can't think straight. Angry tears stung my eyes. I wiped them with my apron and slathered on the icing, then set the table. Bill's keys jingled at the door. Lord, don't let me yell at him and ruin everything. I don't want to fight.

Lord, don't let me yell at him and ruin everything. I don't want to fight.

"I'm home," Bill called from the hall. I brought out the casserole and sat down. He walked in and kissed me on the head. "I think I'm ready for tomorrow," he said. "One area always trips me up, though." He was preoccupied, and we ate in silence.

I cleared our plates and cut two squares of cake. Bill pulled out a textbook. "Can't wait till this last one is over," he said with a sigh.

So he can run off! I dropped our dessert plates on the table and sat hard on my chair. "We're supposed to be in this together," I burst out. "How could you?"

Bill looked up from his book, bewildered.

"I don't want to be treated like yesterday's paper, left behind in this poky apartment while you go off to have a good time with your friends on some stupid golf trip."

"The golf trip?" Bill asked.

"Yes! The trip!" Now I was really crying hard.

He paused, then snapped his textbook shut. "Caroline, why didn't you say something earlier? I'm not a mind reader."

"Don't get snippy with me," I shot back. "This is all your fault, Bill."

"Okay, okay," he said, holding up his hand. "You're right, Caroline. I shouldn't rush off the minute I get a break. I'm sorry. I'll cancel. No problem."

"Now you're trying to make me the bad guy!" I let out everything I had asked the Lord to help me keep in. Every time Bill opened his mouth, I cranked up the volume. "I said I'm sorry. I'll cancel. Didn't you hear me?" I plowed on. "I'm your wife and you don't even know how I feel!" I shouted. "You don't even care."

Bill's face got red. His eyes widened. I'd never seen him this upset. He picked up his butter knife, leaned across the table and sliced my dessert in two! The sagging halves of yellow cake fell flat on the plate in a kind of tired truce. I couldn't believe my eyes.

"You attacked my cake," I said finally. Bill seemed sort of sheepish. "You actually attacked my cake."

Bill nodded, holding back a grin. I didn't. I couldn't any more than I could hold back my anger. I laughed, long and hard. Bill laughed too. We stood up and met beside the table. I nuzzled into him and gazed at our wedding picture again. Marriage doesn't really start until you cut into that perfect-looking cake and get down to the nitty-gritty of daily life and deal with the challenges God brought you together to face. My arms tightened around my husband. We'd survived our first fight. Next time I'd try not to hold out for so long. Better to get it out in the open. But for now

I wanted to enjoy this wonderful feeling. A feeling of being closer now to Bill than ever.

"Tell you what," I said. "Take your golf trip. But next weekend, we have a date at that fancy restaurant across town. Or else." I turned my face toward his, and we kissed like newlyweds. "My treat," Bill said, and he slipped a piece of cake into my mouth.

Caroline Conklin

Hurting goes away; loving—never! It's the best gift the Lord gave us.

Laura Ingalls Wilder

A North Carolina bride's mother was nervous anyway. She stopped off in the ladies room of the Presbyterian church.

When her turn came, all eyes were upon her. And she did look lovely, her pink chiffon gown just a-flowin'.

But in her hand, she was clutching a roll of pink toilet paper. Her pink clutch purse was on the back of the commode.

Margaret G. Bigger

WEDDED CONFUSION

You think things are confusing at your house? In New Philadelphia, Ohio, a double wedding was announced. A nineteen-year-old boy was to marry a sixteen-year-old girl. The groom's seventeen-year-old sister was to wed the father of the bride at the same time.

This means that the sister became her brother's mother-in-law, and the brother became his father-in-law's brother-in-law. His bride became her father's sister-in-law. And their children would be first cousins of the sister-in-law's mother-in-law.

Virgil Schense of Aberdeen, South Dakota, can even top that! He became his father's brother-in-law and the uncle of his three brothers and sisters. His three sisters became nieces of his wife and also her sisters-in-law. His wife became her sister's daughter-in-law's sister-in-law and also her husband's aunt.

Here's how things got that way: Virgil, son of his father's first wife, married the sister of his father's second wife.

"Ah, sweet mystery of life . . ."

Adapted from Lowell Thomas

Marriage means commitment. Of course, so does insanity.

Bernard Brunsting

Marriages begin warm and intimate, but over time they can become cold and businesslike. Consider the seven ages of a marriage cold.

The first year the husband says, "Sugar, I'm worried about my little baby girl. You've got a bad sniffle. I want to put you in the hospital for a complete checkup. I know the food is lousy, but I've arranged for your meals to be sent up from Rossini's. It's all arranged."

The second year: "Listen, honey, I don't like the sound of that cough. I've called Dr. Miller and he's going to rush right over. Now will you go to bed like a good girl just for me, please?"

The third year: "Maybe you'd better lie down, honey. Nothing like a little rest if you're feeling bad. I'll bring you something to eat. Have we got any soup in the house?"

The fourth year: "Look, dear. Be sensible. After you've fed the kids and washed the dishes, you'd better hit the sack."

The fifth year: "Why don't you take a couple of aspirin?"

The sixth year: "If you'd just gargle or something, instead of sitting around barking like a seal . . ."

The seventh year: "For heaven's sake, stop sneezing. What are you trying to do, give me pneumonia?"

Bruce Larson

Cheryl Reimold, an authority on body language, once said, "If you stand up to address a seated person, you gain height and a certain amount of temporary power. But if you face the person directly, on his level (whether sitting or standing), you are more likely to establish communication.

Queen Victoria knew that.

The queen and her husband, Prince Albert, quarreled

about something early in their marriage. Albert walked out of the room and went to his private quarters. Victoria followed, found the door locked, and began pounding on it.

"Who's there?" Prince Albert asked.

"The Queen of England," was the reply. But the door remained locked.

More pounding followed, but then there was a pause. The next sound was that of a gentle tap.

"Who's there?" Albert inquired.

The queen's reply: "Your wife, Albert."

Prince Albert opened the door immediately.

Clifton Fadiman

ON VALENTINE'S DAY

An old man got on a bus one February 14, carrying a dozen roses. He sat beside a young man. The young man looked at the roses and said, "Somebody's going to get a beautiful Valentine's Day gift."

"Yes," said the old man.

A few minutes went by and the old man noticed that his young companion was staring at the roses.

"Do you have a girlfriend?" the old man asked.

"I do," said the young man. "I'm going to see her right now, and I'm going to give her this Valentine's Day card."

They rode in silence for another ten minutes, and then the old man got up to get off the bus. As he stepped out into the aisle, he suddenly placed the roses on the young man's lap and said, "I think my wife would want you to have these. I'll tell her that I gave them to you."

He left the bus quickly. As the bus pulled away, the young man turned to see the old man enter the gates of a cemetery.

Author Unknown

**"My husband gave me a hug for my birthday.
He says 2 arms and 10 fingers count as 12 presents."**

FULL-SERVICE SHOPPING

Jacob, eighty-five, and Rebecca, seventy-nine, were excited about their upcoming wedding. Out for a stroll, they stopped at a drugstore.

Jacob said to the pharmacist, "Do you sell heart medication?"

Pharmacist: "Of course we do."

Jacob: "How about medicine for circulation?"

Pharmacist: "All kinds."

Jacob: "Medicine for rheumatism?"

Pharmacist: "Definitely."

Jacob: "Medicine for memory?"

Pharmacist: "Yes, a large variety."

Jacob: "What about vitamins and sleeping pills?"

Pharmacist: "Absolutely."

Jacob: "You have loose bowel and gas pills?"

Pharmacist: "Yes, with plenty of generics."

Jacob: "What about paraphernalia for diabetes?"

Pharmacist: "Of course. You name any condition, and we have what you need."

Jacob: "Perfect! We'd like to register here for our wedding gifts."

Jim Kraus

FOR LOVE AND ROSES

Comedian Jack Benny, while being one of the funniest actors in our recent history, also had a tender, loving side. He was completely in love with his wife, who stayed by his side for decades, through tough times and terrific times.

When Jack finally "arrived" as a recognized and sought-after comedian, and his financial status soared accordingly, he began sending his lovely wife a single, long-stemmed, red rose every day to thank her for her loyalty and to express his undying love.

This practice went on for many years. Every single day of every week of every year, the beautiful rose arrived faithfully at the door of their home. Even when Jack was out of town or overseas, the roses kept coming, reminding her of his never-failing love and devotion.

When Jack eventually died, his lifelong partner grieved bitterly, as would be expected. Unexpectedly, however, the single red rose continued to be delivered to her every day for over a week after the funeral. Finally, although it seemed so unlikely, she decided the florist was not aware of her husband's death. So she called to inform them that the roses probably should not be sent anymore.

To her surprise, the florist said, "Oh no, Mrs. Benny. Your husband set up a special fund before he died to keep the roses coming to you every day for as long as you live. He wanted you to know that his love was, indeed, undying."

Mary Hollingsworth,

written from public facts

HUSBAND FOR SALE

It happened again. Gene and I were in the car running errands, and I felt he was too close to the car in front of us. As the other automobile slowed down unexpectedly, I shrieked, "Watch out!" Gene slammed on the brakes, and we were jolted forward.

As usual, he had plenty of room to stop, and we could have avoided this jerky reaction if I had kept my mouth

shut. He was angry with me for being a back-seat driver—
again. I told him I screamed because I honestly thought we
were in danger and I believed my warning might save our
lives. He was unconvinced. He pulled
the car to the side of the road, looked
in my direction, and said, "Do you
want to drive?"

Now I was hurt. I wasn't trying to
tell him how to drive. My scream had
been involuntary. I did not plan to make
him feel like an inadequate driver. Tears blocked my vision
as I withdrew into my silent martyr role. (I feel so much
more spiritual when I'm not speaking.) We drove home in
the thick silence of anger, hurt, and misunderstanding.

As we mutely walked into the house, our conflict was
still unresolved. I left Gene in the kitchen and walked into
the next room. Opening my mail, I found this anonymous
letter on my desk:

Now I was hurt. I
wasn't trying to tell
him how to drive.

Dear Friend,

   This letter was started by a woman like yourself
in hopes of bringing relief to other tired and discontented women. Unlike most chain letters, this one
does not cost anything.

   Just bundle up your husband and send him to
the woman whose name appears at the top of the
list. Then add your name to the bottom of the list
and send a copy of this letter to five of your friends

who are equally tired and discontented. When your name comes to the top of the list, you will receive 3,325 men . . . and some of them are bound to be better than the one you gave up!

DO NOT BREAK THIS CHAIN! One woman did, and she received her own jerk back! At this writing, a friend of mine had already received 184 men. They buried her yesterday, but it took four undertakers thirty-six hours to get the smile off her face.

We're counting on you,

A Satisfied Woman

By the time I reached the middle of the letter, I was grinning. As I finished it, I was doubled up in uproarious laughter. My confused husband walked into the room wondering what had transformed his wounded wife. Looking up, my eyes met his. "I'm sorry," I said softly. "I overreacted."

"Me too," he responded, as he slipped an arm around my waist. His lips brushed the side of my face as he whispered in my ear, "Now, what's so funny?" His curiosity was killing him. And I couldn't keep a secret that was this hilarious.

"Listen to this," I said. I read the letter aloud, and both of us fell on the floor laughing until tears ran down our faces.

Carol Kent

Marriage is work—sometimes gritty, sweaty, uncomfortable work. In fact, I figure that the degree of difficulty in combining two lives ranks somewhere between rerouting a hurricane and finding a parking place in downtown Manhattan.

Claire Cloninger and Karla Worley

SUNDAY SURPRISE

A minister was planning a wedding at the close of the Sunday morning service. After the benediction, he had planned to call the couple down to be married in a brief ceremony before the congregation. For the life of him, he couldn't think of the names of those who were to be married.

"Will those wanting to get married please come to the front?" he requested.

Immediately, nine single ladies, three widows, four widowers and six single men stepped to the front.

Tal D. Bonham

WEDDED BLISS

The glances over cocktails
That seem to be so sweet,
Don't seem to be so amorous
Over milk and Shredded Wheat.

Alistair Ross

© 2004 Bunny Hoest. Used by permission.

"Where are your 'I told you so' cards?"

PERKS

E ve...what a perky lady! She definitely had advantages. Stop and think about it. When she and Adam met, she didn't have to wonder, *Is this the right man for me?* She didn't have any immediate concerns if some sweet young thing was vying for her man's attention.

When they were wed, she didn't have to worry about forgetting someone from the invitation list or deciding who the attendants would be. No decisions were necessary on which photographer, caterer or florist. Talk about simplifying life . . .

Guess what? No mother-in-law or father-in-law conflicts. Never once did she have to hear, "Sure wish you could make applesauce like my mom." They never squabbled over whose family they would spend the holidays with.

She never had to worry about ironing Adam's dress shirts or getting the crease straight in his suit pants. There was no friction about Adam not packing up his dirty clothes, at least not in their garden home. Nor did she have to take any ribbing about where she put Adam's lost snakeskin sandals.

Eve was unique. She's the only gal who didn't have to go through puberty, peer pressure or pimples. She didn't go through the agony of handing her parents a bad report card or the knee-knocking experience of trying to explain why she was late getting home. She never once had to hear her parents say, "Why aren't you more like your sister Ethel?"

When she and Adam talked, it wasn't filled with endless tales of the good ol' days and the good ol' boys. Nor did she have to compete with the World Series or the six o'clock Eden news report.

They had a romance, marriage, honeymoon and home life that was made in paradise.

Patsy Clairmont

My friend Jan has an uncle who is ninety-nine years young. He lives in an assisted living facility only because he is legally blind. Otherwise, he is perfectly healthy and capable of taking care of himself. One day several years ago, when he was ninety, she and another friend of ours went to his house to visit him. Jan introduced her friend to him, and he promptly asked if she was single.

Yes, she told him. She was a fifty-six-year-old widow. He then asked if she could drive.

Yes, she said, she could drive. He then asked if she would marry him as he needed a chauffeur.

Well, he didn't get that woman, but at ninety-nine he is still looking.

Rhonda Hogan

© 1998 Randy Glasbergen. www.glasbergen.com

GLASBERGEN

"He's my new boyfriend. I know he's cold and unemotional, but on the other hand, he never criticizes me, he doesn't complain about my friends, and if things don't work out, he'll be gone in the Spring!"

Rev. Gordon McLean, director of the Juvenile Justice Ministry, Metro Chicago Youth for Christ, says he met some interesting neighbors when he moved to a new apartment complex in the Chicago area. One woman told him, "I miss my ex-husband, but my aim is getting better."

Gordon McLean

A man who had just finished one of those marriage books that encourage men to be the head of the home woke up the next morning and told his wife that, from that moment forth, he was going to be in charge, and she would have to obey and meet his every request.

"You're going to cook a real dinner tonight, not something in the microwave, and there will also be a homemade dessert, and when I'm finished eating, you will make my bath, with bubbles, so I can relax. And after that, guess who's going to dress me and comb my hair?"

His wife said, "The funeral director."

Author Unknown

Moonlight and roses are bound to fade
for every lover and every maid;
But the bond that holds in any weather
is learning how to laugh together.

Author Unknown

2

Funny Bone Fitness

*Staying thin and fit is like walking through one
of those fun houses at the fair where the mirrors
are distorted. In one you look tall and thin; in
the next you look short and squatty. When it
comes to weight loss and fitness, you can groan
or giggle about it. We think it's best to just laugh
it off!*

I NEVER MET A COOKIE I DIDN'T FALL IN LOVE WITH

Lead me not into temptation—I can find it myself!
Bumper Sticker

Some people say everyone has a soul mate somewhere
out there. I happen to believe we can have several.
After all, I do—all of them cookies.

I have loved each and every cookie I have ever met,
ever since the time I was big enough to lick the front case

window at my grandmother's bakery in Los Angeles. It was there I was introduced to delicate sugar cookies with maraschino cherries in the middle, sturdy nut bars, and giant, cakelike "moon cookies" with half chocolate, half white icing. But most of all, I loved the chocolate-chip cookies. With my eyes as big as my hips, I'd watch as my grandmother took racks and racks of them out of her brick oven, hot and steamy and gooey. I'd snitch a few into my pocket, stuff a few in my mouth, and pile a bunch into a pink cookie box to take home with me.

Up until now, my undying devotion to cookies, especially chocolate-chip cookies, has known no end. *Give me Mrs. Fields' Chocolate Chunk Macadamia Nut cookies, or give me death!* (And give me a bigger pair of pants while you're at it.)

The other day I reached a breaking point. Actually, it was the zipper on my jeans that reached the breaking point.

Therein lies the problem. As much as I love and adore cookies, which have reciprocated by attaching themselves permanently to my thighs, I'm afraid I've become, um, too big for my britches. The bod isn't what she used to be.

Now, I've been on hundreds of diets in my lifetime, and I've lost hundreds of pounds. Unfortunately, I've also found them all—plus their relatives and friends—and if you ask me, it's getting too crowded in my clothes for all of us. Let's just say it's a strain, especially in the seams of my pants.

The other day I reached a breaking point. Actually, it was

the zipper on my jeans that reached the breaking point. I knew it was time. Despite our four-decade-long love affair, my beloved cookies had become the bane of my existence. It was time for us to part company and go our separate ways.

Sadly, forlornly, I bid them adieu and turned to my bag of mini carrot sticks for solace. However, my heart still yearned for the silky decadence of a chocolate morsel surrounded by buttery crunchiness. *A crumb, just a crumb.* I flipped through the pages of a magazine, fantasizing over the full-color photos of holiday cookies and remembering only the day before when I had eaten my last one (double chocolate mint chunk).

I closed the magazine and prayed, "Lord, lead me not into temptation. My spirit is willing, but this body of mine is so weak!"

My craving subsided for all of three minutes; then it returned. I kept repeating, "It's not a sin to be tempted," as I opened the magazine again and started reading some recipes, waiting for God to give me strength, power and self-control as He led me not into cookie's snare. "It's not a sin to be tempted, it's not a sin to be tempted," I chanted as I sneaked a peak at the recipe for peanut-butter jumbles. *Mmmm, peanut-butter jumbles. Peanut-butter jumbles with chocolate chips. Mmmm.*

I closed my eyes and pictured a chocolate-chip peanut-butter jumble. I imagined the aroma and did my best to recall how it might taste, the whole time congratulating myself on not falling into temptation. Instead of being filled with cookies, I was filled with self-satisfaction. I felt invincible! I was going to beat this hold that cookies had on me—and lose a few pounds in the process.

The next few days were repeats of that first. In the morning, I prayed that the Lord would help me slay this Cookie Monster. Then I spent the rest of the day fighting temptation by studying magazines and cookbook recipes—yet I didn't eat a single cookie (although I did sniff the magazine picture of the blonde brownie bars and lick a bit of brown sugar off the page of the cookbook).

Then came the big test—the Cookie Exchange.

I'd been invited to my friend's cookie party and had looked forward to it for weeks. However, things had changed. Wisdom told me if I didn't go, I could avoid the temptation to eat every cookie in sight, but the more I thought about it, the more sense it made that I should go. That it was *good* for me to go, to look temptation square in the eye and say, "Ha! Gimme your best shot—I'm ready for ya." Yes, I'd prayed for God to "lead me not," but I was confident that He would not let me be tempted beyond what I could bear, and that He would provide a way of escape so I could stand up under it (1 Corinthians 10:13). I actually owed it to Him to prove himself God over my temptation.

Now, despite what some people might say, I'm not a complete idiot. I knew better than to make a batch of cookies from scratch to bring with me. I'd never hold up under that kind of overwhelming temptation. Instead, I decided to buy a package of cookies from the market shelf. Factory-sealed for my protection.

A funny thing happened on my way into the store. I had every intention of going right to the packaged cookie aisle, but my shopping cart took a detour to the refrigerator section where they keep the tubes of cookie dough.

Don't go there, warned the Voice inside my head.

I told the Voice, *But I'm just going to look!* And that's all I did. I looked . . . then ran my fingers down the seam of the package . . . then read the list of ingredients . . . then closed my eyes and tried to imagine the texture of raw dough in my mouth and the degree of bittersweetness in the chocolate chunks. It's not a sin to be tempted, I informed the Voice (before it had a chance to tell me I should drop everything and run).

Thoughts of hot, chewy, gooey cookies, fresh from the oven—for my friends, of course, baked into my mind. *Just think how delighted everyone will be. I owe it to them. Anyone could buy a package of cookies. These would be almost like homemade. Besides, I don't have to eat any. This is strictly an altruistic gesture. I'm doing it for others.*

Up to my elbows in thoughtfulness, I set out to bake. And just in case temptation should try to entice me, I prayed twice for the Lord to lead me not.

The first batch went in the oven without my tasting even one tiny bit. Unless you count the blob of dough that fell on the counter and the chocolate chunk that stuck to the spoon. But everyone knows that doesn't count. Neither do broken cookies (I had to eat three of those), nor burnt ones (two). Plus, as the conscientious friend that I am, I was practically *required* to sample a whole one to make sure they were edible for my friends. That left six cookies out of twelve.

The next batch I dropped on the floor. I had to eat those (after I brushed them off) because we have a terrible problem with ants, and I couldn't throw them in the trash.

The last batch produced six picture-perfect cookies. And four lopsided ones, which everyone knows don't count either, so I ate them as well. The rest of the dough somehow ended up in my mouth, and it wasn't until I'd eaten it that I realized . . . well, that I'd eaten it. But accidental eating doesn't count as "real" eating anyway. In fact, none of my cookie eating qualified as real eating, so technically I didn't succumb to temptation.

Still, I only had thirteen cookies to bring to the Cookie Exchange, and I needed three dozen. By then, I didn't have time to bake any more, even if I'd had another tube of dough. I only had enough time to change into a pair of drawstring pants, finish off the remaining cookies (because of the ant problem), and stop by the store for a package of cookies.

On the way to the Cookie Exchange, I once again prayed for God to "lead me not into temptation." I planned to sip ice water all night and simply enjoy the fellowship—and leave without a plate of cookies. No one would know about my little "episode." Besides, I could always start clean tomorrow.

The first part of the evening went without a hitch. I found a spot near the table with all the cookies on it. It was far enough away that I couldn't touch them, but close enough for me to smell them. Although I'd eaten enough cookies earlier to satisfy the sweet tooth of every past, present, and future human being on earth, I didn't want to miss anything new. *What if someone brought Russian tea cakes? I'd never forgive myself for not getting a taste of those.*

Several times during the evening, friends tried getting me away from my seat to join the party, but it was as if nothing else existed except cookies, glorious cookies. Eventually I did move—closer to the table (so I could rest my water glass). I sniffed; I imagined; I savored; I salivated. I named each cookie. Blessed them. Praised them. *But I did not eat them.*

When everyone had divided the cookies and I had filled the tin I brought (for my family, of course), I said good night and got into my car to return home, duly impressed with myself. I opened the tin of cookies and popped one into my mouth as a congratulatory token.

By the time I arrived home that night, my cookie binge had taken its toll on me. I rolled out of the car with the mother of all bellyaches and staggered to my front door. "Don't let them serve cookies at my funeral," I gasped to my husband as I crawled past him in the hall on my way to my (death) bed.

Nancy Kennedy

I'm on a new tranquilizer diet—I haven't lost an ounce, but I don't care.

Bob Phillips

"Remember the warm-up and the cool-down."

A woman went to the doctor, and he told her she needed to go on a diet.

So he gave her a printed diet to follow and sent her home. Three weeks later she came back, and the doctor was shocked to see that she had gained ten pounds.

"Georgia, what in the world went wrong?"

"I don't know, doctor," she replied. "All I did was eat three meals a day and everything on that diet you gave me."

Mary Hollingsworth

"RULES" OF DIETING

If you drink a diet drink with a chocolate bar, the calories in the chocolate bar are canceled out by the diet drink.

When you eat with someone else, calories don't count if they eat more than you do.

Calories in food used for medicinal purposes never count. Examples: hot chocolate or ice cream.

If you fatten everyone else around you, then you look thinner.

Movie-related foods such as pick 'n' mix and popcorn do not have additional calories because everyone knows that movies aren't real.

When preparing food, things licked off spoons and knives have no calories. Examples: peanut butter on a knife when making a child's sandwich and chocolate cake mix for contribution to school cake sale.

Broken chocolate cookie pieces contain no fat. It leaks out.

Foods that are the same color have the same number of calories, e.g. spinach and pistachio ice cream; mushrooms and white chocolate.

Calories are a unit of heat. Therefore, frozen foods have no calories. Examples include ice cream, frozen pies, and solid chicken nuggets.

Food eaten standing up doesn't count to your daily calorie allowance.

Killy John and Alie Stibbe

In the beginning, there was the word.
And the word was *Chocolate*, and it was good.
Confections 1:5 oz., 240 cal.

Seen on a T-shirt

THE SLIVER

Don't eat a sliver,
Because if you eat a sliver,
You'll want a slice;
And if you eat a slice,
You'll want a slab;
And if you eat a slab,
You're a slob!

Weight Watchers

Desperation is a woman plucking her eyebrows before she steps on the scales.

Killy John and Alie Stibbe

My dress is by Nicole Miller; unfortunately, my body is by cookies 'n' cream.

Mary Hollingsworth

There's a new Chinese diet. Order all the food you want but use only one chopstick.

Bob Monkhouse

A blonde was terribly overweight, so her doctor put her on a diet. "I want you to eat regularly for two days, then skip a day. Repeat this procedure for two weeks. The next time I see you, you'll be at least five pounds lighter."

When the blonde returned two weeks later, the doctor was shocked when she got on the scale. She had lost nearly twenty pounds.

"Why, that's amazing!" the doctor said. "Did you follow my instructions?"

The blonde nodded, then added, "I'll tell you, though, I thought I was going to drop dead every third day."

"From hunger?" asked the doctor.

"No, from skipping."

Jim Kraus

Try to choose foods from the four main food groups: chips, chocolate, Cokes and calcium.

Marie Evans and Ann Shakeshaft

**"Whenever your cholesterol gets too high, a sensor
will send out a signal that automatically locks
the kitchen door and turns on your treadmill."**

TO TELL THE TRUTH

Do you remember the scene from the old *I Love Lucy* show? Lucy and Ethel decided to get part-time jobs, so they went to work in a candy factory. At first it was a breeze because the conveyer belt carrying the pieces of taffy to be wrapped was moving past them very slowly. One at a time, they would pick up a piece of candy, roll it in a wrapper, and twist the ends of the paper, then place the wrapped piece in a box. No problem!

Soon though, the supervisor turned up the speed of the belt, and the candy began coming to them more quickly. In Lucy's looniest fashion, she sped up too. "Come on, Ethel, work faster. We can do this!" So they worked harder and were barely getting the candy wrapped and into the box when . . . the belt sped up again, much faster this time.

Now the candy pieces were coming at them lickety-split!

But not one to give up easily, Lucy was grabbing them by the handfuls, throwing them in the box unwrapped, putting them in her pockets, shoving them in her shirt, and stuffing them in her mouth—anything to keep from being a failure. And anything to keep from getting caught by the supervisor.

But she was just fooling herself. Pretty soon the savvy old supervisor walked in and found Lucy and Ethel with their mouths full of candy and a mess all around them. Caught! They were fired, of course.

> When we're with our friends, we eat salads and fruits. When we're by ourselves, we eat burgers and fries.

That's what a lot of us do when we go on diets, isn't it? We try to fool ourselves and other people. When we're with our friends, we eat salads and fruits. When we're by ourselves, we eat burgers and fries.

So our friends say, "You're really doing well on your diet, aren't you?"

And we say, "Oh yes! I just can't believe how easy this is." Meanwhile, we've gained three pounds.

The thing I finally figured out is this: Even though you can fool your friends and family, and you can even fool yourself, you can't fool your body. Your body will respond to what you really ate, not what you fooled yourself into believing you ate.

If you've ever gone to Weight Watchers, then you know one of the keys to succeeding on that program is to write down what you eat every day—every item, every bite, every morsel. Of course, you can write down anything you want to, even if it's wrong; so if you want to fool yourself, you write down less than what you actually ate. And you're thinking, *Say, I didn't do badly today! See? I only had twenty-six points.*

But you can't fool your body. Your body knows you really ate thirty-five points, and it whispers, "Who are you trying to kid? Here, let me stuff that piece of Snickers Cheesecake over here on your right hip. And I'll just attach that double cheeseburger over here on the left hip. That way, your hips will match nicely in that new pair of one-size-larger jeans you'll have to buy."

And then there's that humiliating trip to weigh in at the meeting. I don't know about you, but I personally think those laughing scales are just plain rude. And that *101 Ways to Make Lime Jello Cookbook* . . .

Faking yourself out when you're dieting is a waist— usually a much bigger waist. Instead of emulating the candy-stuffing *I Love Lucy* show, we'd be better off to pretend that we're playing the old game show called *To Tell the Truth*. Will the real candy wolfer please stand up?

Mary Hollingsworth

HAVE YOUR CAKE AND EAT IT

A woman in our diet club was lamenting that she had gained weight.

She'd made her family's favorite cake over the weekend, she reported, and they'd eaten half of it at dinner.

The next day, she said, she kept staring at the other half until, finally, she cut a thin slice for herself. One slice led to another, and soon the whole cake was gone.

The woman went on to tell us how upset she was with her lack of willpower, and how she knew her husband would be disappointed.

Everyone commiserated until someone asked what her husband said when he found out.

She smiled. "He never found out. I made another cake and ate half!"

Killy John and Abe Stibbe

*"I'm taking you off three things—
breakfast, lunch, and dinner."*

My girlfriend goes to a ladies-only gym called Curves. The name "Curves" is a celebration of a woman's natural body shape, the way God intended. I go to the gym called Chunks.

Basil White

OUCH!

Pain is God's megaphone," C. S. Lewis said.

If that's true, then, folks, I've heard from heaven!

Last year, I went through months that were a literal pain in the neck. I've been accused of being one, and now I know what it feels like to have one.

Our bodies protest when we do things that are beyond their ability to perform.

I hauled too many suitcases, briefcases, purses, word processors and carryons through too many airports and hotel lobbies. I exceeded my recommended load limit, and in doing so, I stretched my back and tendons. I then spent painful months learning the importance of listening to my body.

My physical therapist asked why it took me so long to seek medical help. To tell you the truth, I thought I was just being wimpy, and that if I kept bench pressing my luggage, eventually I would look as fit and fabulous as Stormie Omartian. Instead, I complicated my recovery as the tendon damage spread from my shoulder to my elbow and then to my wrist.

Our bodies protest when we do things that are beyond

their ability to perform. Body signals alert us in many ways. Our muscles, tendons and ligaments scream when we try to lift or carry things that are too heavy.

Les is a strapping fellow who, during his younger years, was so strong (how strong was he?) he could lift a buffalo. What he shouldn't have tried to carry was the two bundles of shingles for our roof. Actually, he might have achieved that hefty task if, after he slung both bags of shingles over his shoulder, he hadn't had to climb up two stories on a ladder. Even then he might have made it if, when he put his foot on the roof, the ladder had stayed still. Which it didn't. And neither did he.

The first part of Les's fall was broken by a porch landing. He then proceeded to tumble down a flight of steps and collide with the less-than-cushy earth.

Stunned, Les lay very still to assess the damage. After a few breathless moments, he rose slowly, slung the bags over his shoulder again, and climbed back up on the roof.

Les's friend Tom Wirsing had witnessed this acrobatic feat. But because Tom was on the roof when it happened and Les took the ladder with him when he fell, Tom couldn't come to Les's aid. He spent several harrowing moments as a helpless bystander. When Les stepped back on the roof, Tom had just two words for him: "Go home!"

The next morning, Les's body was buzzing with messages. Les needed a headset to keep up with all the incoming data. His back went on strike, and his legs, sympathetic to the back's protest, filed their own grievance. Muscles he didn't know were a part of the human structure reported their existence. Bruises the size of roof tiles added color to his battered frame. The bruises served for quite a while like Post-It notes, as a reminder never to do that again.

Along with Post-It notes, our bodies have built-in alarm clocks. Instead of waking us up, they're designed to insist on rest. These alarms go off every time we nod dangerously behind a steering wheel, we fall asleep in class, or we drag through a day with the enthusiasm of a yawn.

When Les and I were a young married couple (versus the relics we are today), Les worked a long way from home. One morning, as he neared work, he began to nod. We had stayed up late that week, and his need to sleep sat on his eyes like sandbags. The sound of the early-morning traffic became a lullaby, and Les took a nap. It didn't last long. He woke abruptly when he hit a parked car, which hit a parked car, which hit another parked car.

Les called me on a pay phone from the scene of the crash. "Patsy, I've been in an accident."

"Are you okay?"

"I'm not sure. My head is bleeding. Here come the police. I have to go." And he hung up.

I was seven months pregnant and beside myself with concern. I had no idea where the accident happened or if he truly was all right. My body soon announced that if I didn't settle down, our family would be having more than an accident.

Five hours later, my smiling husband walked in the

door. I hugged him and cried with relief. Then I wanted to lambaste him for not calling me back. It all worked out well. Les decided it was easier to hit the hay than a lineup of cars.

Mood swings can be the body's beeper, reporting possible hormonal havoc. I remember three sisters I met at a retreat who were concerned their fourth sister was in spiritual trouble because she wasn't her usual bouncy self. They kept her up late at night and prayed with her over every possible hidden sin in her life. Later, they found out she was pregnant. After a couple of months and some uninterrupted sleep, her hormones settled down, and she was back to her perky self.

I'm not saying the all-night vigil was a bad idea, but there are times when mood swings beep attention to a legitimate health issue.

There's no doubt we are fearfully and wonderfully made. All we have to do is listen to our bodies and respond with good choices. Some of you already are disciplined and wise in caring for yourselves. But, like me, many of you don't listen until you're in trouble. We could all benefit by answering the following:

How much water do you drink in a day? (No fair counting the water in coffee or cola.)

How many hours of sleep do you require a night to feel "normal"? (Les requires seven hours but prefers six. I need eight hours but enjoy nine. Les catapults from the bed each morning, while I have to be jump-started just to ignite a pulse.)

Do you have an exercise regimen? (Getting out of bed each morning does not qualify as weight lifting.)

When was your last eye exam? (I took my mangled glasses in last week for repair. I had sat on them . . . for the third time. The woman looked at them and said, "Lady, do you know which end these were made for?"

"Evidently not," I replied sweetly, "or I wouldn't be here again.")

Write down the date of your last dental appointment. (If BC follows the date, it has been too long.)

Are you listening to your body when it says, "Enough is enough" (food, work, rest)?

When was your last physical? (Talking to a friend who once took a first-aid course does not count.)

Did it include a pap smear? (This is an uplifting experience.)

Have you had a mammogram? (That's where the technician thinks she's a magician and tries to turn a cup into saucer.)

Have you ever had a change in your weight without a change in your eating? (My mother-in-law thought she was fat. Her "fat" turned out to be a tumor the size of a watermelon. My husband was losing weight while eating like a buffalo. It turned out he was diabetic.)

Are you having frequent headaches, stomachaches, backaches, rashes, sleeplessness, spotting, mood swings, urination, unquenchable thirst and so on? It's time to find out why.

How many pills do you take in a week? In a month? Are you masking a growing health issue? (Our plop-plop, fizz-fizz mentality covers our pain but doesn't resolve it.)

Trust the way God has designed your body to let you know when you need to make a life adjustment or a visit to your family doctor. This body is just a temporary time suit. (Can't you hear it ticking?) It's the only one we get before heaven's new, improved version, which will be complete with eternal vision.

Speaking of vision, remember that in this life, your glasses belong on your nose. Take it from someone who knows.

Patsy Clairmont

I hear there's a new diet-while-you-sleep pill. What great news! I'll take a dozen, and you can wake me when I'm a size eight.

Mary Hollingsworth

"Rats!" the man said to his pal while weighing himself at the drugstore.

"What's wrong?" asked his friend.

"I began this diet yesterday, but the scale says I'm heavier. Here, Norm, hold my jacket . . . It still says I'm heavier. Here, hold my shoes. I'm still heavier. Here, hold my Twinkies."

Kevin Pagan

YEAR-ROUND COMMITMENT

When Gene Smith left our office at five o'clock on a sunny Tuesday afternoon, he was his usual likable self. Thirteen hours later this mild-mannered teddy bear of a man had morphed into a frenzied, diet-obsessed maniac. I may never know what happened while Gene was away. I only know that he returned an obnoxious cheerleader for a healthy lifestyle. Good information? Absolutely! But how could he have become an overnight nutritional expert? Gene was suddenly determined to drop a few of the extra pounds he—like so many of us—carried. Fine, but how could he be so disgustingly vivacious about beginning a diet? Especially so early in the morning?

Gene was suddenly determined to drop a few of the extra pounds he—like so many of us—carried.

I don't do mornings. On a good morning, I am quiet, reserved and can even be a tad grumpy. My mood grows even worse when a normally easygoing friend suddenly resembles Richard Simmons on speed, complete with rampant enthusiasm and unsolicited advice.

"You need to drink eight glasses of water each day to hydrate and cleanse your body of impurities," Gene preached.

"Eat at least five servings of fruits and vegetables daily. I am going to eat fruit and maybe just a poached egg for breakfast."

Please, someone shut him up so I can eat my Mrs. Winner's Cinnamon Swirl in peace.

"Cathy, you really should drink juice instead of Diet Coke," Gene suggested.

He stepped back when I looked up from my desk with a steely-eyed glare of irritation combined with hormone-induced hunger and morning grumpiness. Gene recognized that look as dangerous. He quietly sulked away to share his diet diatribe with Russell and Mike, our very tall and thin co-workers in this small family-like company.

I turned to the mass of paperwork occupying my desktop. While I typed letters, signed contracts and made phone calls, I occasionally heard Gene's words—*carbs, fat grams, leafy vegetables*—wafting through the building followed by groans from Russell and Mike.

Noon arrived before I looked up from my desk.

"Hey, I'm going for a quick lunch at Waffle House. Anyone want to go?" I asked.

"Can I go?" Gene asked timidly. "I'll even drive."

I responded with my usual tenderness, "Sure, but you had better use your mouth just for eating. I don't need a diet discourse at Waffle House."

We took a booth near the door and a server quickly approached our table. Gene ordered a salad. He really seemed committed to his diet. I was proud of him.

The server took my order, but before she could leave, Gene cried, "Wait! I'm not finished!"

I assumed he wanted crackers or a glass of water. Instead, he spoke with calm resolve: "I want a double cheeseburger, a double order of hashbrowns, scattered—covered—smothered, and a bowl of chili." The waitress smiled and turned to leave as Gene added, "And a waffle!"

A waffle? Salad, cheeseburger, hashbrowns, chili, and . . . a waffle?

We stared at Gene during a moment of awkward silence before I finally spoke. "You will have to excuse him, ma'am," I explained. "He has been dieting for about four hours and is crazy with hunger."

Gene enjoyed every bite of his lunch and was a little sheepish the rest of the day. He seemed to be having trouble digesting his chili/waffle combo.

Cathy Lee Phillips

My doctor says I must give up those little intimate dinners for two unless I have someone eating with me.

Henny Youngman

MY FAVORITE THOUGHTS ON EXERCISE

I had to give up jogging for my health. My thighs kept running together and setting my pantyhose on fire.

Amazing! You just hang something in your closet for a while, and it shrinks two sizes.

Inside some of us is a thin person struggling to get out, but she can usually be sedated with a few pieces of chocolate cake.

Becky Freeman

A TOUCHING STORY OF LOVE AND MARRIAGE

An elderly man lay dying in his bed. In death's agony, he suddenly smelled the aroma of his favorite chocolate chip cookies wafting up the stairs. He gathered his remaining strength and lifted himself from the bed. Leaning against the wall, he slowly made his way out of the bedroom. With even greater effort, he forced his bony fingers to grab the handrail and let himself down the stairs, one stumbling set at a time.

With labored breath, he leaned against the door frame, gazing into the kitchen. Were it not for death's agony, he would have thought himself already in heaven. There, on the kitchen table, spread out in rows upon wax paper, were literally hundreds of his favorite chocolate chip cookies. Was it heaven? Or was it one final act of heroic love from his devoted wife of sixty years, seeing to it that he left this world a happy man?

Mustering one great final effort, he threw himself toward the table, landing on his knees in a rumpled posture. His parched lips were slightly parted. The wondrous taste of the cookie was already in his mouth, seemingly bringing him back to life. The aged and withered hand, driven by one last gritty effort, shakingly made its way towards a cookie at the edge of the table, when it was suddenly smacked with a spatula by his wife. "Stay out of those," she said, "they're for the funeral!"

Author Unknown

THIN PEOPLE DON'T

I read every diet I can get my hands on. I even follow their suggestions. But eventually, inevitably, I always get fat again. Now, at last, I've found The Answer. After living for almost fourteen years with a man who never gains an ounce no matter what I serve him, I've found out what it is that keeps him thin. He thinks differently. The real difference between fat people and thin people is that thin people:

Avoid eating popcorn in the movies because it gets their hands greasy;

Split a large combination pizza with three friends;

Think Oreo cookies are for kids;

Nibble cashews one at a time;

Think that doughnuts are indigestible;

Read books they have to hold with both hands;

Become so absorbed in a weekend project they forget to have lunch;

Fill the candy dish on their desks with paper clips;

Counteract the midafternoon slump with a nap instead of a cinnamon Danish;

Exchange the deep fryer they received for Christmas for a clock radio;

Lose their appetites when they're depressed;

Think chocolate Easter bunnies are for kids;

Save leftovers that are too skimpy to use for another meal in order to make interesting soups;

Throw out stale potato chips;

Will eat only Swiss or Dutch chocolate, which cannot be found except in a special store;

Think it's too much trouble to stop at a special store just to buy chocolate;

Don't celebrate with a hot-fudge sundae every time they lose a pound;

Warm up after skiing with black coffee instead of hot chocolate and whipped cream;

Try all the salads at the buffet, leaving room for only one dessert;

Find iced tea more refreshing than an ice-cream soda;

Get into such interesting conversations at cocktail parties that they never quite work their way over to the hors-d'oeuvre table;

Have no compulsion to keep the candy dish symmetrical by reducing the jelly beans to an equal number of each color;

Think that topping brownies with ice cream makes too rich a dessert;

Bring four cookies into the TV room instead of a box;

Think banana splits are for kids.

Barbara Florio Graham

TO EXERCISE OR NOT TO EXERCISE

It is well documented that for every mile you jog, you add one minute to your life. This enables you, at age eighty-five, to spend an additional five months in a nursing home at five thousand dollars per month.

My grandmother started walking five miles a day when she was sixty. She is now seventy, and we don't know where she is.

The only reason I would take up jogging is so that I could hear heavy breathing again.

I joined a health club last year, spent about four hundred dollars. Haven't lost a pound. Apparently, you have to show up.

I don't exercise at all. If God meant us to touch our toes, He would have put them further up our body.

I like long walks, especially when they are taken by people who annoy me.

I have flabby thighs, but fortunately my stomach covers them.

The advantage of exercising every day is that you die healthier.

If you are going to try cross-country skiing, start with a small country.

And last, but not least, I don't jog—it makes the ice jump right out of my glass.

The Poddy's Directory

SITTING ON THE PARK BENCH, WATCHING ALL THE FOLKS JOG BY

Recently, my friend Linda suggested the two of us begin a regular walking program. We're both writers and tend to spend a lot of time sitting at the typewriter. That's not to say we're out of shape. Why, just this morning I lifted seventy-pound weights for ten minutes. (It took me that long to get them off my chest.) And last Tuesday I went roller skating all day. (Actually, I only intended to skate for one hour, but I couldn't figure out how to stop.) I do pretty well on my stationary bicycle too—or at least I thought I did until someone pointed out that the pedals weren't the part that's supposed to stay stationary.

Like most people, though, I don't get all the exercise I need. I should probably spend more time on my rowing machine, but every time I put it in my swimming pool, it sinks. (I'm trying to learn how to hold my breath longer, but so far I haven't been able to get more than one or two pulls on the row in.) I even went shopping for a treadmill, but I couldn't find one with a "saunter" button.

> A walking program, however, sounded like something I could keep up with, so I agreed to give it a try.

A walking program, however, sounded like something I could keep up with, so I agreed to give it a try.

We decided to meet every Monday, Wednesday, and Friday morning and walk five or six laps around a local park. I tried changing it to five or six laps around the drinking fountain, but my friend felt we needed to get our blood circulating again. It had stayed sluggish long enough.

Our first lap went fine. We noticed an ambulance circling (someone must have tipped them off), but we refused to let that intimidate us. We even showed off and sprinted once, but unfortunately, the ice cream truck got away.

The third lap was a bit more difficult. Our feet hurt, our legs ached, we were breathing hard and walking so slowly I'm surprised our pedometers didn't clock us at "coma" speed.

By the fifth lap, we were ready to flag down the ambulance, but it had already left on another call.

"How 'bout taking a break?" I pleaded as several seniors effortlessly jogged by. "Let's face it, the park statues are moving faster than we are."

Eyeing a bench off to the side, we made a dash—no, a slow trot—okay, a crawl for it, and sat there the rest of the morning catching our breath.

"You know," Linda said when the color finally returned to her cheeks, "sitting here watching everyone else walk or jog by isn't helping us any. We're not burning off any calories or working a single muscle in our bodies."

"You're right. You're absolutely right," I said, wiping my brow with my shirt sleeve. "Let's start waving at them too."

Martha Bolton

3

Animal Antics

*Fuzzy and feisty, cuddly and cute—we're crazy
about our pets and animals! They're our furry
kids, and we adore them . . . just as they do us.
Animals can be endearing, challenging, pesky
and precious. Their antics leave us rolling off
the sofa or shaking our heads in disbelief. What
would we do without them?*

THE CAT WHO CAME BACK

I was foraging in the general store on my usual monthly
run into town when a voice seemed to just barge into my
thoughts: *Michael, why don't you pick up a few cans . . . just
in case?* I was standing in front of a shelf full of cat food.
Just in case of what? I wondered. Just in case that darn
stray cat came sniffing around my place again? If I was
going to do anything with a can of cat food, I would probably throw it at him. I'd moved way out here in the middle of
nowhere—a twelve-mile truck drive, then six more miles
via snowmobile from town—so no one would bother me.

But the urge to buy cat food kept at me. Finally, I picked up a few cans and shoved them in with the rest of my groceries. I headed for the register.

I dreaded this part. I'd have to stand there while the girl rang me up. Sure, she was used to me, never asked questions. But it was uncomfortable standing there while she eyeballed each and every item, like I was being x-rayed or something. The cat food. That would get her attention.

I stared at the wall above her head, down at the floor, at my hands.

"You got a cat?" she asked, her eyebrows arched as she rang up the cans.

"Nope," I said. Her face red, she went back to bagging my things without saying another word. Probably thought I was trying to stretch my food dollar.

I paid for my stuff, piled into my pickup and hit the long, snowy road home. Home was a cabin I'd built myself, from scratch, using money from a small inheritance and some of my savings. My nearest neighbor—a real nice lady named Ina Rae—was two miles away. Close enough.

If I sound like a fellow who'd given up on life, well, that's not quite true. I'd given up on people. I suppose it started when I was small. My parents were kind of rough on me. I'd hide out in my room and stay below the radar. If this was the way people who were supposed to love you treated you, then just imagine how the rest of the world must be, animals included. And God? Well, when you give up on people you kind of give up on him too. I guess.

I graduated high school by the skin of my teeth. College? Yeah, right. I hit the road and didn't look back. I hadn't talked to my folks since. In fact, I didn't even know where they lived anymore.

I worked a whole bunch of jobs, eventually settling in as a janitor at a school. People left me alone unless something needed fixing. I made sure things stayed fixed. Sometimes I'd go down to the boiler room or into an empty classroom and read. One of my favorite books was *Walden* by Henry David Thoreau. Thoreau sought meaning by living alone in a cabin on a lake. That appealed to me. Self-discovery. No one to answer to. No one to talk to. Just me.

I traveled: Alaska, British Columbia, the Yukon, all over the Northwest. Eventually, I got to Sandpoint, in northern Idaho, and decided to stick around for a while. I found myself a nice spot of land and built my own Walden. There was something in the air here, just a nice feeling. Peaceful.

There was nothing better than sitting out on the deck and kicking back. I'd look at the mountains, the clouds and the pine trees until my mind got quiet and all I could hear was the babbling creek. Times like that, it was almost like I just dissolved into the air.

One cold day when the air froze your breath as soon as you exhaled, something under the picnic table caught my eye—a splash of gray against the winter white. I stooped over for a better look. A cat. "Shoo!" I yelled. The critter looked up at me. I stamped my foot and yelled again. The cat shot off the deck and disappeared.

How the heck did a little cat get out here in the middle of nowhere anyway? I wondered. Well, it wasn't my problem, and I wasn't taking in boarders.

All right, then. So how come I'd just bought cat food? I couldn't come up with an answer. I stopped the pickup and transferred everything into my snowmobile. I still had another six miles to go.

Yep, I really was in the middle of nowhere. Once in a while, I'd run into Ina Rae. She knew not to ask me too many questions. *Maybe you could get her to come take the cat,* I thought.

The snowmobile bounced along, jarring me back to my senses. *Get Ina Rae to take the cat? And then be caught up with her always telling you about how it's doing, asking if you want to visit? No way.* It was bad enough I had to deal with people in town once a month.

I finally reached my cabin. No sign of the cat. I put away my provisions, shaking my head at myself for wasting good money on cat food.

Next morning, there he was, out on the deck. Just a ball of gray fur. He wasn't moving. I walked over. Was he dead? No. Still breathing. I couldn't just leave him out there. I cradled him close to my chest, carried him inside and sat down next to the stove. His fur was covered with ice. After a while, he opened his eyes and stretched a bit. Then he reached a paw out toward me.

"Hey," I said, shaking it.

I set out the cat food in a bowl next to some water. He

was wary at first, but when he finally dug in, he practically licked the dish clean. I let him be while I did some chores. Frankly, I wondered how I'd ever get rid of him now. Then, just like that, he was gone. I felt panicky. "Here, cat!" I called from the deck. I went back in and searched all over. No cat.

Fine, I told myself. *Better that he doesn't start depending on you anyway.*

He came back, though, scratching at the door. That night, he jumped up onto the bed and settled down on my pillow. "Get out of here! It's bad enough I took you in. You are not sleeping with me!" I nudged the cat off the bed. He jumped right back on. The only way I got any sleep was to give in and let him stay.

The next morning I decided that maybe Ina Rae could give me some advice.

"Michael, what a surprise!" she said when I showed up at her door.

"I found this cat," I told her, "and he's driving me nuts."

"Cats are all different," she told me. "But don't worry; he'll let you know what he needs. And he'll settle in eventually."

"He'd better not," I said. "Come spring, he's gone."

One morning I awoke to a quiet rumbling, like an outboard motor way off in the distance, as peaceful a sound as I'd ever heard. I lay back and just let it kind of vibrate through me, and for the first time in years I found myself thinking of my parents. Finally I turned my head. The cat was curled in a ball, eyes closed, purring contentedly.

"What am I gonna call you?" I asked him. "Can't keep saying 'cat' all the time." I went through a bunch of possibilities, finally settling on Jake.

Jake slept next to my head every night. He followed me on walks in the woods and nestled in my lap while I sat out on the deck. Ina Rae told me how happy I looked. Once she wouldn't have dreamed of saying such a thing.

The time for my monthly supply run came. I loaded up on cat food. The poor checkout girl probably thought I'd developed a taste for it. Taking a big breath, I gave her the news. "I got a cat. His name's Jake." It was the first time in a long time I'd told anyone a thing about myself. . . . Just a simple, insignificant fact, but for me it was a momentous occasion.

> It felt like I'd opened a window and let some fresh air in.

You know something? It felt good. It felt like I'd opened a window and let some fresh air in. And I found myself saying a little prayer. *Thanks, God, for sending me that little cat. You knew I needed someone like Jake. You knew it all along, I bet.* Now I was anxious to get home to my cat.

Plowing through the backwoods of Idaho on my snowmobile, I couldn't help but think of how beautiful everything looked, almost as if I hadn't noticed it before. I really did live an isolated existence. Even Thoreau eventually rejoined society. Maybe other people weren't so bad after all, at least in small doses. I mean, look how wrong I'd been about cats.

And while I was at it, maybe I could track down my folks and give them a ring.

Michael Sowders

A CAT'S HEAVEN

St. Peter is standing at heaven's pearly gates when a cat shows up. "You were a loving cat on earth," says St. Peter, "so I want to give you one special thing you have always wanted."

"Well, I did always want a nice satin pillow like my master had, so I could lie on it."

"That's easy," St. Peter replied. "We will have a satin pillow ready for you."

Next, a family of mice appears at the pearly gates.

St. Peter says, "Ah, I remember you. You were good mice on earth. You didn't steal food from anyone's house and never hurt other animals. Therefore, I want to grant you one special wish."

The father mouse replied, "Well, we always watched the children skating, and it looked like fun. Could we each have some skates, please?"

"Granted. You shall have your wish."

The next day, St. Peter saw the cat sunning itself on the pillow. "Well, cat, how's the satin pillow?"

"Absolutely wonderful," the cat replied. "And say, those 'Meals on Wheels' were an extra nice touch too!"

Jim Kraus

Outside of a dog, a book is a man's best friend.
Inside a dog, it's too dark to read.

Groucho Marx

DOG DICTIONARY

Bicycles: Two-wheeled exercise machines invented
for dogs to control body fat. To get maximum aerobic
benefit, hide behind a bush. When you spot one, dash
out, bark loudly and run alongside for a few yards.
The human on the bike will swerve and fall into the
bushes.

Deafness: This malady kicks in when your human calls.
Symptoms include either running in the opposite
direction or simply lying down.

Thunder: This is a signal that the world is coming
to an end. Humans remain amazingly calm during
thunderstorms, so it is necessary to warn them of the
danger by trembling uncontrollably, panting, rolling
your eyes wildly, whimpering or barking incessantly,
and never letting them out of your sight.

Wastebasket: This is a doggie treasure chest regularly
stocked with a changing array of interesting things.
When you get bored, turn the basket over and strew
the contents all over the house. When your human

comes home, they're sure to express their excitement with your creative decorating.

Bath: This is a process by which humans drench the floor, walls and themselves with your help. For added fun, shake vigorously and frequently.

Bump: The best way to get your human's attention when they are drinking a hot cup of coffee or tea.

Goosebump: A last-resort maneuver to use when the Bump doesn't get the attention you require.

Lean: Every good dog's response to the command "Sit," especially if your human is dressed for an evening out. Incredibly effective before black-tie events. Your hair adds a personal touch to the outfit.

Love: A feeling of intense affection, given freely and without restriction. Show your love by wagging your tail and giving slobbery kisses. If you're lucky, a human will love you in return.

Sofas: This is your doggie napkin. After eating, it is polite to run up and down the front of the sofa and wipe your face clean.

Dog bed: Any soft, clean surface, such as the white bedspread in the guest room or the newly upholstered couch in the living room.

Drool: What you do when your human has food and you don't. To do this properly, you must sit as close as you can, look sad and let the drool fall on their shoes, or better yet, on their lap.

Garbage can: An aromatic container that your neighbors put out once a week to test your ingenuity. Stand on your hind legs and push the lid off. If you do it right, you are rewarded with paper to shred, bones to consume and stale pieces of bread to scatter throughout the neighborhood.

Leash: A strap that attaches to your collar, enabling you to lead your human everywhere you want him or her to go.

Jim Kraus

PRINCESS FUR-FACE

Whad'ya say we change the furniture around?" Ken queried one Saturday morning as we were finishing our last cups of coffee/tea. "Let's put the couch by the window and the two chairs facing the fireplace." I had learned years before to trust Ken's fine eye for furniture placement.

"Sounds good to me, babe," I said, "but do you have the stamina for Ashley's neurotic response?"

Ashley was our cocker spaniel, who reacted strongly

against all visual changes. She wanted things to remain in their accustomed spots. If they didn't, she had one of her "spells." It didn't matter how big or small the change; each warranted a protest. Let me give you an example.

A friend popped in on me one morning and, for some reason, just dropped her purse in the middle of the floor as we made our way to the "chat chairs" by the window. (This was before the rearrangement.) Several moments later Ashley, who hated to miss anything, came trotting into the room. Spotting my friend's purse in the middle of the floor, she skidded to a stiff-legged halt, stared briefly at the purse and went into a dramatic fit of barking. Slowly circling the purse, she barked, growled and scowled until my friend finally placed her purse behind the chair. Gradually, Ashley settled down, but it was obvious the visit was ruined for her.

As Ken pondered the price to be paid for furniture rearrangement, he noted that Ashley was out on the deck dozing in the sun. She might not notice what was going on until the dastardly deed was done.

Several hours later, Ashley roused herself from her siesta and ambled into the house. She immediately assessed that unauthorized changes had occurred in her absence. After barking herself nearly hoarse, she flounced out of the living room and stayed in her "sleep area" for several days. We delivered her food and water. Gradually, she came to realize that the couch was now in a far better spot for her because she was able to see out the window. (Of course, she was allowed on the furniture!) This made it possible for her to visually patrol the neighborhood without leaving the comforts of home.

Perhaps the greatest trauma Princess Fur-Face had to endure was when we got a new car. Ashley's sleep area was in a small room adjoining the garage, and although the car wasn't fully visible to her, it was in close proximity.

On the first night of their cohabitation, Ashley, who had not yet been introduced to the new car, scampered down the stairs to bed as was her custom. We stood behind the closed door holding our breath. No sound ... no barking ... no response at all. Ken's theory was that because it was dark, Ashley couldn't see the car. Our intention was to later, in the daylight, gradually coax her into an accepting relationship with the new vehicle.

Around 1:00 AM, we were awakened by the sound of frantic, ferocious barking. Ashley had discovered the car. Fearing she'd disturb the neighbors, Ken flew down the stairs, scooped up Ashley along with her bed, and deposited her in our room, something Ken normally refused to do. She grumbled and complained the rest of the night, but at least she didn't bark.

Because Ken drove the car to work during the day, I had no opportunity to ease Ashley into a spirit of charitableness about the car. Each night she seemed to forget about the alien in the garage when she first went to bed, and then rediscover it sometime after midnight.

At 2:00 AM on the fourth night of Ashley's histrionics, Ken exasperatedly dragged himself out of bed and announced he had just come up with a plan, which required that we both get dressed and take Ashley for a ride.

"Are you going to dump her out of the car somewhere in another county?" I asked cautiously as I threw on jeans and a sweatshirt.

"Trust me" was all he said.

Ken thrust a squirming, growling, barking cocker into my arms, and we got in the monster car to begin what Ken said would be the "taming ride." For at least an hour, Ashley was a bundle of growling rigidity in my arms. With the radio playing soft music and both of us stroking Ashley with words of love and encouragement (none of which we felt at that moment), Ashley began to relax. An hour and a half later and miles from home, she went limp in my arms and fell asleep. From that moment on, Ashley had peace about her metal roommate. In fact, one of her favorite activities became riding in the car.

I hate to tell you how closely I identify with Ashley at times. There are God-gifts I have fought so fervently only to find that once I yield my resisting spirit, I reap incredible benefits. For example, I certainly don't overly resist the concept of grace, but I've tried to earn it a million times. I seem to tenaciously cling to the mistaken notion that I've got to be good enough in order to deserve grace. How many times does God have to hold my rigidly resisting spirit until finally, with celestial music in my ears, I relax and embrace his gift?

Ashley learned with just one ride.

Marilyn Meberg

"First my ball rolled under the sofa, then my water dish was too warm, then the squeaker broke on my rubber pork chop. I've had a horrible day and I'm totally stressed out!!!"

10 OBSERVATIONS FOR VISITORS
WHO COMPLAIN ABOUT MY PET

My pet lives here. You don't.

If you don't want his hair on your clothes, stay off the furniture. (Why do you think they call it "fur"niture?)

I like my pet a lot better than I like most people. So, watch it!

To you, my pet is an animal. To me, my pet is an adopted child, who happens to be short, hairy and walks on all fours. (Nobody is perfect!) Although he doesn't speak English, he communicates with me extremely well. We understand each other . . . which is more than I can say for most people I know.

Don't feel bad, my pet growls at me too. He doesn't bite me, but as for you . . .

My pet kills spiders, mice, roaches and other unwanted vermin for me. What can you do to help me?

When I come home, my pet is always excited to see me. He bounds around the room with glee, barks wildly, wags his tail and brings me a toy to show how thrilled he is that I'm home. When was the last time you demonstrated your happiness to see me?

My pet is happy to eat leftovers—even slightly furry ones. You, on the other hand, expect me to cook. Duh!

My pet goes outside to use the bathroom. I never have to clean a toilet after him. But are you that considerate? Noooo. You insist on going inside the house. You don't even put the seat down, Sweetie!

In summary, dogs and cats are better than kids. They eat less, don't ask for money all the time, are easier to train, usually come when called (this does not apply to cats), never drive your car, don't hang out with drug-using friends, don't smoke or drink, don't worry about having to buy the latest fashions, don't wear your clothes, and don't need a jillion dollars for college. Also, if they get pregnant, you can sell the children!

A. Nony Mous
Expanded by Mary Hollingsworth

Teach your children to brush their teeth, brush their hair and brush the dog . . . but not with the same brush. The dog resents it.

Author Unknown

I WANNA BE A BEAR . . .

If you're a bear, you get to hibernate. You do nothing but sleep for six months. I could deal with that. Before you hibernate, you're supposed to eat yourself stupid. I could deal with that, too.

If you're a bear, you birth your children (who are the size of walnuts) while you're sleeping and wake to partially grown, cute cuddly cubs. I could definitely deal with that.

If you're a mama bear, everyone knows you mean business. You swat anyone who bothers your cubs. If your cubs get out of line, you swat them too. I could deal with that.

If you're a bear, your mate EXPECTS you to wake up growling. He EXPECTS that you will have hairy legs and excess body fat.

Yup . . . I wanna be a bear.

Author Unknown

DAISY

The following personals ad appeared in a newspaper:

SBF (Single Black Female) seeks male companionship, ethnicity unimportant.

I'm a svelte, good-looking girl who LOVES to play. I love long walks in the woods. Hunting. Camping. Riding in your pickup truck.

Fishing trips. Cozy winter nights spent lying by the fire. Candlelight dinners will have me eating out of your hand. Rub me the right way and watch me respond. I'll be at the front door when you get home from work, wearing only what nature gave me. Kiss me and I'm yours.

Call 555-2121 and ask for Daisy.

The phone number was for the Humane Society. Daisy was an eight-week-old black labrador retriever.

Author Unknown

CHIPPIE

Chippie the budgie never saw it coming. One second, he was peacefully perched in his cage. The next, he was sucked in, washed up and blown over.

The problems began when Chippie's owner decided to clean Chippie's cage with a vacuum cleaner. She removed the attachment from the end of the hose and stuck it in the cage. The phone rang and she turned to pick it up. She'd barely said "Hello" when ssopp! Chippie got sucked in.

The bird owner gasped, put down the phone, turned off the vacuum and opened the bag. There was Chippie—still alive but stunned.

Since the bird was covered in dust, she grabbed him and raced to the bathroom, turned on the tap and held Chippie under the running water. Then, realizing that Chippie was soaked and shivering, she did what any compassionate bird owner would do—she reached for the hair dryer and blasted the pet with hot air.

Poor Chippie never knew what hit him.

A few days after the trauma, the reporter who'd initially written about the event contacted Chippie's owner to see how the bird was recovering. "Well," she replied, "Chippie doesn't sing much anymore—he just sits and stares."

It's not difficult to see why.

J. John and Mark Stibbe

I like pigs. Dogs look up to us, cats look down on us, but pigs treat us as equals.

Winston Churchill

If a pig loses its voice, is it disgruntled?

Author Unknown

CANARY CAPER

Once a year, on Valentine's Day, Mama paired the male and female birds and asked God's blessing on their union. Come spring, dozens of baby canaries hatched, and

we moved all the families to the aviary my daddy had built in the garden. Christian picked out a nice shady spot where he could watch the canaries fly around in the big structure wrapped in wire netting.

Then one afternoon Mama called urgently: "I forgot to close the latch on the aviary door! Some of the birds have escaped!" I rushed outside. "They're only babies," Mama cried. "They're sure to get lost or hurt!" At that moment Christian got up from his place in the shade and stretched. *Or eaten,* I thought.

We crept slowly to two yellow birds peeking out of a bush. "Stay there," I whispered, as Mama advanced with the net. She brought it down with a whoosh, but the birds flew right out from under it in a flash.

"Where'd they go?" she asked.

"There's one!" I called, spotting a shot of yellow in a tree. "And there! And there!" Canaries were everywhere! Mama ran back and forth with her net as Christian fixed his gaze on one hapless creature perched on a low branch. Our cat crouched low to the ground, ready to pounce.

"No!" Mama cried, but Christian sprang through the air and snatched the baby bird in his jaws. I covered my eyes. I couldn't watch. It was too gruesome even to imagine.

"My, oh my!" Mama said. Strangely enough, I heard relief in her voice.

I peeked through my fingers. Mama was just putting the captured bird back in its cage as the cat caught another one! Christian padded over to Mama and ever so gently placed the frightened ball of feathers in her hands. Then he rescued another.

When he had seen all the escaped canaries safely home, Christian lay back down in the shade. I'd say he was smiling —like the cat who didn't eat the canaries.

Myrtle "Cookie" Potter

A man followed a woman and her dog out of a movie theater. He stopped her and said, "I'm sorry to bother you, but I couldn't help noticing that your dog was really into the movie. He cried at the right spots and fidgeted in his seat at the boring parts. Most of all, he laughed like crazy at the funny parts. Did you find that unusual?"

"Yes," she replied, "because he hated the book!"

Jim Kraus

THE FAMILY CIRCUS®   **By Bil Keane**

©1999
BKI

"I like dogs 'cause if you're doing something stupid,
they don't yell at you. They do it with you."

JUST A WALK IN THE PARK

The zoo security guard pulled his light green Plymouth Valiant to an abrupt halt as he approached the aquatics section. There in the lengthening shadows of early evening was a large male chimpanzee walking slowly toward the back of the California sea lion exhibit. The guard had been at the zoo long enough to recognize that this was Toto. The zoo had eight chimpanzees in the collection. Of the eight, Toto was the worst possible chimp to be three quarters of a mile from his cage. He was a former circus chimp and, in all likelihood, he had been badly abused. By human standards,

Toto was crazy, psychotic, totally unpredictable. He would be gentle and friendly one moment and frenzied and violent the next.

The security guard rolled up his window and locked all the car doors. He reached for his walkie-talkie. He clicked it to the "on" position, and it crackled to life. With his eyes fixed on the chimp, which was now walking slowly toward his vehicle, he pressed the "send" button and whispered, "Sam, this is Joey . . . you there?"

He lifted the button and heard Sam reply, "Yeah, I'm here. What's up? Sounds like you're looking at a ghost . . . over."

"I wish I were. I'm in back of the chief keeper's shack just below the California sea lion exhibit, looking at Toto . . . over."

"Sounds like we have a problem. I'll notify the acting director and the capture team. Do your best to keep track of his whereabouts. Keep me posted. And Joey, be real careful. From what I've heard, Toto is bad news."

Joey kept track of Toto, and for whatever reason, Toto stayed near the chief's shack. He was, for all intents and purposes, lost. His zoo cage had been his territory for two years and, without help, he would not be able to find his way back to it. Not knowing where he was, Toto was left with the problem of having nowhere to run. In his tangled mind, he imagined he could be in enemy-occupied territory and was on the verge of emotional frenzy. He probably stayed in the area to be near the security guard who was keeping an eye on him.

Most of the capture team arrived at the same time and wisely stayed in their cars, waiting for Dr. Gale, the assistant director. Dr. Gale was an excellent animal-capture man worth waiting for, and the truth was that he would not have tolerated it any other way.

Toto was preoccupied with the sounds and smells of the immediate area and was satisfied that his company was staying in their cars. When Dr. Gale arrived, it was very dark, and only the horizon gave a hint that the sun had just set for the night. The zoo's dark green shrubbery nearly absorbed Toto's silhouette, and only his occasional movement betrayed his whereabouts. Dr. Gale directed the security guard to watch Toto, then motioned for the capture team to follow him out of the area. Once out of Toto's sight, they got out of their cars and listened to Dr. Gale's plan.

"We can't dart Toto with the capture gun; it is too dark to know if we hit him. He might fall into a pool, or worst of all, we may miss and scare him so that he leaves the zoo. Then he'd need to be shot before he hurt someone in the local neighborhood. If any of you have change, give it to me." They looked at each other, wondering what Dr. Gale had up his sleeve. But they knew him well enough not to question him. The change added up to a little less than two dollars. Dr. Gale sighed as he held it in his hand. He gave Bob Spellings fifty cents of it and told him to run and get a Coke from the nearest vending machine. He told the other men to drive up to the zoo's health center, open all the doors, and wait there for him and Toto. He told them he was going to attempt to walk Toto back to his cage; but he felt the fewer animal-care staff that Toto saw, the less chance there would be of Toto's flipping out and becoming violent.

Bob Spelling returned with the Coke and handed it to Dr. Gale, who took a sip and smiled a "wish-me-luck" smile. He waited for the men to clear the area, then walked slowly toward Toto. When he was nearing the escaped chimp he could see that Toto was a bit apprehensive, and even in the dark he could see that Toto was beginning to stand; his hair was on end, and he looked as if he were about to charge.

Dr. Gale spoke softly, "You want something to drink, Toto?" Toto settled down and walked slowly forward and looked briefly at the cup and then into Dr. Gale's eyes. He reached for the man's hand and pulled it and the cup to his mouth and moaned contentedly. He poured most of the cup into his mouth. Dr. Gale was wishing the zoo served larger Cokes because his plan was to lure him from vending machine to vending machine until they reached Toto's cage. But if Toto were going to finish everything so quickly, he might not follow to the next reward. Even worse, he might want more, and there would be no more to give him. It never took much to disturb Toto, and that was the last thing Dr. Gale wanted to happen alone in the dark in the middle of the zoo. He was already questioning the wisdom of his own plan and looked around to see if any of the men were still nearby to suggest Plan B. But he was alone. He wasn't really alone: There was a psychotic former circus chimp standing at his side drinking the last drop of Coke out of a cup that seemed smaller than ever.

Dr. Gale saw the chief keeper's building and concluded that he might buy some time if he could lock Toto in the building. So he offered Toto his hand, and Toto took it—something he would have done as a young chimp but may not do for long as an old chimp who was six times as strong as the man who was leading him. Dr. Gale removed his keys from his pocket and unlocked the chief keeper's office. He walked into the dark office, hoping Toto would follow. He did. It was darker inside than out and Dr. Gale waited until he was sure Toto was fully inside.

Then Dr. Gale made a quick move and slipped out the door as quickly as he could. He slammed the door and locked it. His heart was pounding and beads of perspiration were forming on his forehead. He wiped it with his handkerchief and walked on his tiptoes to see if Toto was calmly inside.

> His heart was pounding and beads of perspiration were forming on his forehead.

He shaded his eyes from the glare of the street light that created reflections on the window and stared into the darkness of the office. He strained his eyes to see Toto, but could not locate the chimp. He felt a hand on his shoulder and slowly turned to find himself face to face with a disturbed Toto. In a mimicking fashion, Toto was also shielding his eyes from the reflection as he, too, stared into the darkness, trying to discover what had frightened the doctor out of the office.

"Let's go home, Toto," said the doctor, resigned to the first plan. Toto followed him to the next vending machine where he purchased a small box of Good and Plenty candies. Toto enjoyed them immensely, but he would stop, sit down and suck on them, so progress was somewhat impeded. Dr. Gale was limited to one more purchase, and he was not even half way to the health center. The wizened vet noticed a drinking fountain and turned the handle to show Toto that he could get a drink. Toto drank copious drafts of water and was captured by the novelty of the drinking device.

A lion roared from its night quarters. Toto stood straight up and rocked back and forth as if he were going to begin an aggressive display. He ran toward the lion and screamed one loud scream as a warning to his unseen enemy. Then he looked back at Dr. Gale as if to say, "Well, I guess that takes care of that." Dr. Gale praised him in a soft voice and rewarded him with a Good and Plenty.

The Good and Plenty ran out, so he made one last purchase. A Payday candy bar slid out of the vending machine. Toto watched with interest as its wrapper was peeled away and a small piece was handed to him. Dr. Gale walked faster now, knowing he was on borrowed time. Toto grunted a "wait for me" sound and ran on all fours to catch up. The Payday was clearly a favorite choice. The chimp tugged at his benefactor's pant leg for another piece. Progress was now at a sufficient pace, and it looked as though they might make it to the health center after all.

As they rounded the corner at the mountain zebra exhibit, a terror-filled event took place. Ed Alonzo, the principal keeper, was waiting fifty yards away under a street light, monitoring the doctor's journey. If Dr. Gale got in trouble, Ed wanted to be there to help. But now Ed was in trouble. When Toto saw Ed under the street light, he stood up and hooted. He bolted away from Dr. Gale and ran at full speed toward the frozen principal keeper. Toto had injured others, and Ed fully expected to be bitten and beaten within an inch of his life, so he braced himself for the attack.

Toto looked menacing as he charged closer and closer. Ed swallowed and prepared himself for the awesome impact he was about to experience. At the last possible second, Toto pulled up short and stood up in front of Ed to greet him. Ed had been his keeper a few years before, and Toto was merely saying hello with a great deal of enthusiasm. Seeing a person that Toto remembered fondly had thoroughly piqued his interest. He had grown tired of the night's adventure, and Ed probably represented care and security. Toto reached for Ed's hand, which was shaking noticeably from the massive dose of adrenaline, which had just been released into his system. The baton had been handed to Ed, so the last hundred yards were his to accomplish.

He and Toto walked up a narrow overgrown path, and when they reached the top, they could see the health center in full view. Toto released Ed's hand and again ran full speed until he had entered the health center's surgery door. He walked down the well-lighted hallway into the cage room and stood peering through the open door of his cage as if he were trying to make up his mind, "Shall I go in, or shall I stay out?" It was at this point that Bill Dickman, a brave and foolish keeper, ran full swing into Toto, bumping him into his cage and slamming the door behind him. Toto hooted his displeasure, but he decided to be forgiving because he was so glad to be home.

Gary Richmond

A DOG'S PLEA

Treat me kindly, my beloved friend, for no heart in all the world is more grateful for kindness than the loving heart of me.

Do not break my spirit with a stick, for though I might lick your hand between blows, your patience and understanding will more quickly teach me the things you would have me learn.

Speak to me often, for your voice is the world's sweetest music, as you must know by the fierce wagging of my tail when your footstep falls upon my waiting ear.

Please take me inside when it is cold and wet, for I am a domesticated animal, no longer accustomed to bitter elements. I ask no greater glory than the privilege of sitting at your feet beside the hearth.

Keep my pan filled with fresh water, for I cannot tell you when I suffer thirst.

Feed me clean food that I may stay well, to romp and play and do your bidding, to walk by your side and stand ready, willing and able to protect you with my life should your life be in danger.

And, my friend, when I am very old, and I no longer enjoy good health, hearing and sight, do not make heroic efforts to keep me going. I am not having any fun. Please see that my trusting life is taken gently. I shall leave this earth knowing with the last breath I draw that my fate was always safest in your hands.

Author Unknown

Heaven will not ever heaven be unless my pet is there to welcome me.

Epitaph in a Pet Cemetery

4

On the Highway to Humor

Traveling around our wonderful world gives rise to both laudable and laughable incidents. Driving on the other side of the road, converting currencies, figuring out what time it is, eating culturally diverse (and sometimes puzzling) foods, learning to haggle with shopkeepers—all these experiences and more become delightful memories in our life scrapbooks.

WORKING GIRL

Sometimes I amaze myself. I have an uncanny ability to get into desperate situations, especially on business trips. Here's a case in point. After a full day of book promoting, I finished my last television spot in Denver. As I hurriedly packed my autumn dog-and-pony show for my coauthored book, *A Mother's Manual for Holiday Survival*, it crossed my mind that I resembled part of the road crew from Ringling Brothers Circus. I thought about professional women who travel with a laptop computer and leather briefcase. Instead of a portfolio of important papers, I travel with five bags full of fall squash candle holders, a new-potato wreath, decorated pumpkins, hurricane lantern, pomegranates, fall leaves, pine cones and Pilgrim hats filled with popcorn and candy corn. I lugged my bags to the rental car, knowing I'd best get to the airport fast or else I'd miss my plane.

I climbed into the unfamiliar car and found the wind-shield wipers, radio, defroster, air conditioner, hazard lights and hood release before finally locating the head-lights. When I turned the ignition key, the seat belt closed around me like an Indiana Jones booby trap. (I have a few choice words for the idiot in Detroit who invented those belts.) I hate being at the mercy of a high-tech car. To make matters worse, I didn't have a clue as to how to get to the air-port, and I only had forty-five minutes to get there.

> After a five-second hair fluff, lipstick touch-up and squirt of perfume, I made my move.

About that time, a Federal Express truck pulled up in front of me. Ah . . . who else would better know the streets of Denver, I thought. *I'll use the old damsel-in-distress approach.* After a five-second hair fluff, lipstick touch-up and squirt of perfume, I made my move. As the car with-drew its tentacles, I jumped out and approached the driver. "Excuse me, sir," I used my most helpless feminine voice. "I wonder if you could tell me how to get to the airport?"

Unimpressed with my charm, he hardly glanced up, then

answered in one breath, "SureTakeEleventheasttoBroadway thengonorthtwoblockstoColfaxtoUniversitytheneastonMLK andfollowthesigns . . . you can't miss it." He jumped in his truck and sped off to make his next delivery deadline.

"Okay, Kathy, you have a college degree," I said to myself. "No problemo." I took off.

After traveling eight blocks, the reality of my situation hit. Trust me, you don't know fear until you've been in a strange city after dark, driving a rental car in rush-hour traffic in a snowstorm, only to find yourself in the adult-only district of downtown not knowing whether you're getting closer to the airport or farther from it. To my left, I saw a line of people standing in the snow waiting for the doors to open for the female mud wrestling match between Daring Dee Dee and Tantalizing Tanya. And the theater marquee on my right read, "The Escapades of Luscious Lolita." I envisioned the following morning's headline: Budding Authoress Assaulted Outside X-rated Peep Show After Wrecking Rental Car. Investigators Unable To Explain Tentacle Marks Across Her Chest.

Spotting a policeman two lanes over, I dodged a patch of ice and two lanes of traffic to chase him down. I pulled in front of his patrol car and stopped at a red light. Wondering what moving violation I could commit, I thought, *What have I got to lose? A jail cell would be safer than where I am right now.* I leapt from my car and ran back to the police car and asked for directions. He spurted out a few highway numbers then pointed at the green light to remind me I was holding up fifty cars. I ran back to my car, jumped in and sped off. Involuntarily, I took the scenic route and arrived at the airport three minutes before my plane was scheduled to take off—only to learn it had been delayed. Thanks to the snowstorm in Denver and tornadoes in Dallas, I could now sit down and have a coronary at leisure.

Kathy Peel

TOP TEN AIRLINE ANNOUNCEMENTS

10. Thank you for flying Delta Business Express. We hope you enjoyed giving us the business as much as we enjoyed taking you for a ride!

9. Your seat cushion can be used for flotation. In the event of an emergency water landing, please take the cushion—compliments of Reno Air.

8. As you exit the plane, make sure to gather all of your belongings. Anything left behind will be distributed evenly among the flight attendants. Please don't leave children or spouses.

7. Welcome aboard Southwest Airlines. In the event of a sudden loss of cabin pressure, oxygen masks will descend from the ceiling. Stop screaming, and place it over your face.

6. As you exit, please remember—there may be fifty ways to leave your lover, but there are only four ways out of this airplane!

5. After a high-speed landing in Phoenix: "Whoa, big
    fella. Whoa!"

4. Thanks for choosing TWA. We ask you to please
    remain seated as Captain Kangaroo bounces us to
    the terminal.

3. This is a nonsmoking flight. If you must smoke,
    please step out on the wing and watch our in-flight
    movie *Gone with the Wind*.

2. Thank you for flying the friendly skies of United.
    Last one off the plane cleans it!

1. At American Airlines, we are pleased to have some
    of the best flight attendants in the industry.
    Unfortunately, none are on this flight.

Author Unknown

LESSON FROM A PENGUIN

I've spent the majority of my career as a traveling sale-
man, and I know that much of a salesman's free time on
the road is spent battling loneliness. There's not a sorrier
bunch anywhere than a group of salesmen eating their dinners alone in a hotel coffee shop. But one year, my little daughter, Jeanine, gave me the antidote for my homesickness.

It had black beady eyes, a red bow tie and orange feet
—a stuffed toy penguin that stood about five inches tall.

Attached to its left wing with paste (still wet when I tore away the wrapping) was a wooden sign bearing the hand-painted declaration, "I Love My Dad!" I immediately granted it a place of honor on my dresser.

One morning when I was packing for a trip, I tossed the penguin in my suitcase. That night when I called home, Jeanine was distraught that the penguin had disappeared. "Honey, it's here with me. I brought it on my trip." That news pleased her considerably.

Henceforth the penguin came with me—as essential as my briefcase or shaving kit. And we made friends. In Albuquerque, New Mexico, I checked into my hotel, dumped out my bag and dashed to a meeting. When I returned, the maid had turned down the bed and propped the penguin on the pillow.

In Boston, I found it perched in a fresh drinking glass on the nightstand (the penguin had trouble standing upright). The next morning I left it sitting in a chair. Again that night, it was in the glass. I think these maids didn't want me to forget the penguin's message: I Love My Dad!

One night I discovered the penguin missing, and after a frantic phone call, I learned I'd left it in my previous hotel room, where it had been rescued by a heroic maid. I drove a hundred miles to retrieve it, arriving near midnight. The penguin was waiting at the front desk. In the lobby, tired business travelers looked on at the reunion—I like to think with a touch of envy. One guy smiled and another shook my hand.

Once a bemused customs agent at Kennedy Airport in

New York dug the penguin out of my suitcase and, holding it up, said, "Thank God we don't charge a tax on love or you'd owe a bundle."

> "Thank God we don't charge a tax on love or you'd owe a bundle."

Jeanine is a college student now, and I don't travel as much. The penguin is back on my dresser. But it is still a reminder that love is a wonderful traveling companion. All those years on the road, it was the one thing I never left home without.

Edmund Boyle

MURPHY'S LAWS FOR FREQUENT FLYERS

No flight ever leaves on time unless you are running late and need the delay to make the flight.

If you are running late for a flight, it will depart from the farthest gate within the terminal.

If you arrive very early for a flight, it inevitably will be delayed.

Flights never leave from Gate #1 at any terminal in the world.

If you must work on your flight, you will experience turbulence as soon as you touch pen to paper.

If you are assigned a middle seat, you can determine who has the seats on the aisle and the window while you are still in the boarding area. Just look for the two largest passengers.

Only passengers seated in window seats ever have to get up to go to the lavatory.

The crying baby on board your flight is always seated next to you.

The best-looking woman on your flight is never seated next to you.

The less carry-on luggage space available on an aircraft, the more carry-on luggage passengers will bring aboard.

Author Unknown

After a lengthy delay at the gate while waiting to depart, the Captain finally came on the PA system and announced: "I'm sorry for the delay, but the machine that smashes your baggage and removes the handles is broken, so the ground crew is having to do it all by hand today!"

Martin Leeuwis

CAMP RUN-A-MOK

The next time I tell you I am going to vacation at a mountain camp, please shoot me. A "friend" told me about this quaint little family camp that was just amazing and insisted I would never forget it. She was right. I won't ever forget it. I imagined fun-filled days and restful, quiet nights in the fresh air. It was just what my family needed. It didn't quite work out that way.

We packed the car and headed for the majestic Rocky Mountains, but our enthusiasm got curbed when we broke down in front of a federal prison, right in front of the "Caution: Don't pick up hitchhikers here!" sign. It was 106 degrees out, but the good Lord sent an angel to push us to safety. This angel was missing a few teeth and smoked Camels, but I think it was just part of the disguise. We limped to the nearest small town and fixed the car while I had a soda on a bench in front of a convenience store. There were a few "angels" on that bench, too!

We eventually got to "Camp Run-A-Mok." It was built in the 1950s. That was also when my cabin was last vacuumed. Our cabin-mates on the other side of the rice-paper wall were elderly with little or no hearing. They yelled, snored and snorted all night. Finally, after midnight, my husband politely knocked on the door and asked them to quiet down. Their reply was classic: "Oh, you can HEAR us?" This from the couple who was registering 7.6 on the Richter scale. I had brought my white noise machine with me, on the off chance I would need it. It has several soothing settings like babbling brook, rain and the ocean to lull me into dreamland. I had that sucker cranked to "tornado," but to no avail. I tossed restlessly all night and dreamed of sinusy old people vacuuming. No worry. Tomorrow would be another day.

"Alrighty! We'll have a beautiful day, chock full of fun," I giggled to myself. We went to the bowling alley. Only two of the four lanes worked, but no bother. On my first try, I got a strike. Things were looking up. On my next throw, my ball suddenly veered to the right, then left. After a double take, I discovered that my ball had a couple of chips. Did I say chips? I meant CHUNKS missing! All of the balls did, so I resigned myself to the fact that on each throw, my ball would scurry down the alley like a water beetle. I bowled like Wilma Flintstone. Oh well. There was always the ropes course . . .

The ropes course! I had done these before! Tension wires suspended sixty feet above the ground . . . zip cords just waiting for me to jump from one tree to the next, speeding through the air like Lara Croft, Tomb Raider! I could hardly wait. We went to the course, but couldn't find it because we were looking up in the trees. This ropes course was two feet off the ground and was based on teamwork and "trust" exercises, like falling backwards and catching each other. Yippee. At this point, my idea of teamwork would be all of us swallowing our cyanide pills at the same time. I gritted my teeth and tried to stay positive. After all, there was always horseback riding.

> I gritted my teeth and tried to stay positive.

I went to the stable to see the fine steed that would whisk me across the meadows, my hair flying in slow motion like a TV commercial. I imagined looking up into the sculpted face of the magnificent beast that would carry me off into nature. Then I saw it. I had to look down, but I saw it: this short, swaybacked, beaten-down poor excuse for a horse. Even the glue factory passed on this one. It slowly glanced up at me, chewing a wad of old hay. It had the look in its eye that let me know it would scrape me off its back the minute any tree was in reach. Realizing that my beautiful designer cowboy boots would drag on the ground, ruining them for all future country theme parties, I opted out of horseback riding. Okay, so much for that. There was always swimming.

We all got ready—swimsuits, beach towels, snorkels, fins and sunscreen. Bring on the pool! We ran to the water slide, but no water was running. Not wanting to tear off all of my skin at one time, I decided that we would just play in the pool at the bottom. I have seen pea soup with more clarity! I asked a camp counselor what the deal was, and he informed me that it was pond water. I swear I saw a water moccasin swim by and heard two leeches talking about "the other white meat." Knowing this was an ear infection waiting to happen, we passed.

That evening, we were almost treated to "country" music, complete with a washboard and jug, but we hid in the trees and escaped. A counselor found us sneaking around the campground and informed us that it was skit time! I threw myself down in the dirt and feigned a seizure to avoid going. Okay, maybe I am exaggerating, but I would have if she insisted . . .

Another night of snoring, throat-clearing, cupboard slamming, toilet flushing, and it was morning. At breakfast, we were treated to a couple of parents congratulating their children on graduating from high school. Tears flowed, poems were read and cameras clicked to preserve the memory for eternity. Darn it all, I just couldn't muster up any emotion, so I sat there and drank the entire pot of coffee myself.

We only lasted thirty-six hours at that camp. I think we left skid marks on our way out. The next time a "friend" tells me where to go for a vacation, I won't be listening.

Zarette Beard

"Here's the shortcut I was telling you about."

HEAD 'EM UP, MOVE 'EM OUT!

In the late 1970s, we lived in Monroe, Louisiana, where my husband and I worked with the university church. It was called the university church because it was located directly across the street from Northeast Louisiana University. And we loved working with the energetic and inquisitive college students and interacting with the talented and knowledgeable faculty members who attended the church.

Louisiana is an interesting place to live and travel. And because my husband taught training classes for churches throughout the state, we were often on the road going to and coming from his appointments.

Now that doesn't seem like a big deal, does it? And in most any other state, it wouldn't have been. But in Louisiana, it's a whole other story.

You see, in those days in Louisiana, they had what was called the Open Range Law. And believe me, when they said "open range," they meant it. In other words, cattle and horses could roam anywhere they wanted to because many places had no fences. It was "open range."

"So what?" you ask. So the small, two-lane Louisiana state highways often ran right through the open range. You'd be trucking along at sixty miles per hour, and suddenly two or three cattle would wander out into the road unannounced. Screech! And you'd do a double back flip trying to stop before you hit them.

By the way, did I think to say that if you did hit them, it was your fault? And you were required to pay damages to the owner of the animal you hit, not to mention the damage done to your vehicle.

Okay, so you had to watch out for cattle, right? Yes, and that was particularly entertaining at night when it was pitch black, there was a bayou on either side of the road, and there were no shoulders on the road. You'd be sailing along, making good time, when suddenly in the inky night your headlights would illuminate the funny shapes of the ears and horns of a whole herd of cattle nonchalantly bedded down in the middle of the highway. Screech!

I'll bet you're wondering why the cattle were on the highway.

I'll bet you're wondering why the cattle were on the highway. Good question! It seems that the asphalt soaked up the sun in the daytime; so, at night, the road was warmer than the cold ground. The cattle simply chose the heated asphalt to stay warm. And again, if you hit them, it was your fault and your expense.

So my husband and I were zipping along the highway on our way home from a training one night, and we came upon a herd of cattle in the road. We managed to get stopped without running over them, but now what? Bayous on each side of the road, no shoulders to go around them, can't go through them. What to do?

My husband, having been raised on a cattle farm in Kansas, had a better idea of what to do than I did, being strictly a city girl. So he inched up closer to the cattle and began beeping the horn and flashing the lights. He rolled down his window and began calling to the cattle, urging them to move out of the way. Slowly, one at a time, they began to hoist themselves up and meander off the road, bawling and mooing their complaints as they went. And we crept forward a little at a time as the openings allowed. Eventually, we came out on the other side of the herd and could travel on.

Looking back, I saw the cattle wandering back to the road where they resumed their former places for the night.

I felt like Rowdy Yates on *Rawhide*. "Head 'em up, move 'em out!" Not something I would expect to have to say from the plush front seats of your Chrysler New Yorker on a public highway, but an incident that brought a quirky smile to my face just the same.

Mary Hollingsworth

TRAVEL LANGUAGE

Tour Guide Says:	Translation:
Old world charm	No bath
Tropical	Rainy
Majestic setting	A long way from town
Options galore	Nothing is included in the itinerary
Secluded hideaway	Impossible to find or get to
Preregistered room	Already occupied
Explore on your own	Pay for it yourself
Knowledgeable hosts	They've flown in an airplane before
No extra fees	No extras

Tour Guide Says:	Translation:
Nominal fee	Outrageous charge
Standard	Substandard
Deluxe	Standard
Superior	One free shower cap
All the amenities	Two free shower caps
Plush	Top and bottom sheets
Gentle breezes	Occasional gale-force winds
Light and airy	No air conditioning
Picturesque	Noisy theme park next door

Jim Kraus

10 WAYS TO KNOW YOUR FAMILY VACATION WAS A SUCCESS

1. All your children are still alive (broken bones and missing teeth don't count).

2. The car still has at least two hubcaps and one bumper (bent ones count).

3. The two traffic tickets you got in California total slightly less than the national debt.

4. The aroma of baby poop has almost dissipated from the car seat.

5. You still have one complete pair of flip flops between the five of you (never mind that one is size nine and one is size three).

6. You were able to salvage almost all the clothes your three-year-old tried to flush down the motel toilet.

7. You can now refold a road map in less than an hour.

8. Your husband is still speaking to you, even if it is under his breath and between clenched teeth.

9. You can still see a McDonald's sign and not throw up.

10. The last time your four-year-old asked, "Are we there yet?" you were able to say, "Yes! Yes! Thank you, God. Yes!"

Mary Hollingsworth

For Pete's sake. Try not to look so much like a tourist, Fred.

A man in a tour group thought he had mastered French well enough to speak for himself. With his guide standing by, he approached a couple of Parisians and struck up an eloquent conversation. The locals, however, didn't respond to his questions. At length, the villagers began conversing with each other in low voices.

"I give up," the tourist admitted to the guide. "What are they saying?"

"They're debating whether you were speaking English or German."

Dan Harmon

A BITTER WELCOME

It was my first time to travel abroad. I was twenty years old and had taken a temporary job to work in South Africa. I was to live with a local hunting guide and shoot video for a low-budget TV show. The job didn't pay much; actually, I think I came out in the red that summer. But having the chance to travel and thinking that I knew everything prevailed. The funny thing about twenty-year-olds is that they will do anything just to prove they can. That is what got the better of me on this trip.

> The funny thing about twenty-year-olds is that they will do anything just to prove they can.

I was the only American living there for the season. The rest of the Americans would come and go in two-week segments. Vacationing, hunting and shopping all crammed in a tornado of a schedule. No real time for getting to know the natives or appreciating the culture or heritage. I, on the other hand, had plenty of time to get to know them, and now that I look back, appreciate that they have a much simpler way of living. To live in South Africa is to work and survive, but always make time for family and friends, and never know a stranger.

Three days after my arrival in the alien land, I was lying in my little dormitory bedroom taking a minute to write in my journal when J.P., the guide I was living with, came in and asked for a minute of my time. He then proceeded to tell me he would like it if we could do a segment about local heritage. It was a great idea; my producers would see that I went beyond their expectations. I quickly grabbed my camera and gear. J.P. suggested that we start in the garden and talk about the native aloe plant that grew up to eighteen feet tall. I set up the camera on the tripod, hooked up all the microphones, and did a check that everything was working properly.

The shot was beautiful; it was going to be me on the left side and J.P. on the right. Behind us was an aloe plant that was six feet tall. Behind that were the rolling hills of the South African landscape. Open, peaceful, and very serene, it would work nicely. The look was believable and would draw people to really listen and see what we would be talking about.

All the workers, guides, trackers and even a few small

children started gathering around. I should have thought this unusual, but maybe they just wanted to see what all the fuss was about in the compound of the homestead of the ranch. By the time we started, there was no doubt that we had drawn an audience, most of whom were talking in Afrikaans, smiling and giggling. Of course, they were just excited about being on American TV. Just look at the way people act in America whenever there is a TV camera around; that had to have been it.

J.P. suggested that I start the conversation because I was the American. So, now standing in front of a couple of dozen locals and a recording camera, I started by introducing myself and then J.P. I made a little small talk about how lovely everything was in the stunning country. Then I asked J.P. to tell me about the aloe plant behind us. He started talking about how the aloe that grew in Africa was different than those grown in America. They both had healing properties and both had a green ooze; the African variety tasted amazing.

He told about growing up in the rural areas of the country and how his mother would treat him and his two brothers to aloe milkshakes. J.P. then even let us in on the secret recipe: one aloe leaf, half a cup of sugar, milk and ice cream. He talked about how it was a nostalgic part of his childhood.

It was during his story when J.P. reached behind us and broke off a piece of the aloe. He ended his story and made an offer of good faith by presenting me the green, gooey leaf. It looked rancid and smelled about the same. But J.P. told me to try it and see what I thought. Having an audience and a camera rolling, I did not want to go through the hassle of a second take. So I raised the leaf to my mouth and bit down and started chewing. It only took seconds for me to realize that what I had just done was the biggest mistake of my life. A taste more bitter than anything I could have imagined ran into my mouth (a taste that tainted everything I tried to eat or drink for the next several days). I then doubled over spitting and gagging. My fellow cohost doubled over as well, but his was in laughter that he couldn't contain. The audience, who I thought were there to see how American TV is made, were also laughing hysterically.

It seems that I wasn't the first to fall for the aloe milkshake. And, boy, did I fall hard. For the rest of my time in Africa, people would ask me how the aloe was. It was a bitter welcome. So if ever in Africa, never listen to anyone who tries to tell you that they eat aloe.

Gabe Hogan

CHILD'S PLAY

Once a child was sitting on a great log that lay by the roadside, playing; and another child came along, and stopped to speak to him.

"What are you doing?" asked the second child.

"I am sailing to the Southern seas," replied the first, "to get a cargo of monkeys and elephant tusks and crystal balls as large as oranges. Come up here, and you may sail with me if you like."

So the second child climbed upon the log.

"Look!" said the first child. "See how the foam bubbles up before the ship, and trails and floats away behind! Look! The water is so clear that we can see the fishes swimming about, blue and red and green. There goes a parrotfish; my father told me about them. I should not wonder if we saw a whale in about a minute."

"What are you talking about?" asked the second child, peevishly.

"There is no water here, only grass; and anyhow this is nothing but a log. You cannot get to islands in this way."

"But we *have* got to them," cried the first child. "We are at them now. I see the palm trees waving, and the white sand glittering. Look! There are the natives gathering to welcome us on the beach. They have feather cloaks and necklaces and anklets of copper as red as gold. Oh! And there is an elephant coming straight toward us."

"I should think you would be ashamed," said the second child. "That is Widow Slocum."

"It's all the same," said the first child.

Presently, the second child got down from the log.

"I am going to play stick-knife," he said. "I don't see any sense in this. I think you are pretty dull to play things that aren't really there." And he walked slowly away.

The first child looked after him a moment.

"I think you are pretty dull," he said to himself, "to see nothing but what is under your nose."

But he was too well mannered to say this aloud; and having taken in his cargo, he sailed for another port.

Laura E. Richards

THAT'S MY SEAT

A man edged his way down the aisle to what he thought was his row aboard a jetliner awaiting takeoff. He looked at his ticket, then at the gentleman sitting by the window, then back at his ticket, then back at the gentleman.

"I have 17-F," he stated, getting the other's attention. "I believe you're in my seat."

"No, I'm in 17-D. Says so right here." He took out his own ticket and showed it to the man in the aisle.

"Yes, but 17-D is the aisle seat. You see, the seating runs from side to side, A-B-C and then D-E-F. A and F are the window seats, and C and D are the aisle seats."

"Nonsense. I asked them for a window seat, so this must be it. Seat 17-D, flight 501 to St. Louis."

"Oh. Then you're definitely out of place. All the seats going to St. Louis are in the middle row."

Dan Harmon

There's a book that tells you where you should go on your vacation. It's called your checkbook.

Author Unknown

A large commercial jet was flying from Chicago to Los Angeles. About an hour after takeoff, the passengers on board heard a voice over the loudspeaker. It began: "This is a recording. You have the privilege of being on the first wholly electronically controlled jet. The plane took off electronically. It is now flying at forty thousand feet electronically. And it will land in Los Angeles electronically.

"This plane has no pilot, it has no copilot, and no flight engineer because they are no longer needed. But do not worry, nothing can possibly go wrong . . . go wrong . . . go wrong . . . go wrong . . . go wrong."

James C. Humes

"Relax, Dad . . . it's macaroni."

THE GREAT UNDERWEAR ESCAPADE

In the late 1970s, we were living in Monroe, Louisiana. My husband's brother, Loren, his wife, Penny, and their four children were then working as missionaries in Bangkok, Thailand. In June, we got word that they were coming home for a visit.

The problem was, the cost of flying a family of six from Bangkok to Wichita, Kansas, was astronomical. So, to save them a lot of money, I agreed to drive our fifteen-passenger Dodge Maxiwagon from Monroe to San Francisco, pick them up at the airport, and transport them back to Kansas to the Hollingsworth family farm. Then I would drive back to Monroe from there. The round trip would be about five thousand miles.

To make the trip more fun for me, I invited my friend Ouida to go with me, and she agreed. She was a teacher in Arlington, Texas, and was out for summer vacation. So a road trip sounded like fun to her too.

When the time came, I packed up the van and drove to Arlington (about a six-hour trip), spent the night at Ouida's, and we left the next morning, California bound—quite an adventure for us.

The trip to San Francisco went well; we had no hiccups in our travels, and we enjoyed the variegated passing scenery along the way, listened to our favorite music, and relived old memories from our history as friends. We arrived in San Francisco three days later, road weary, but in good spirits. When we crossed the Golden Gate Bridge, it felt as if we had entered the Promised Land after wandering in the desert.

The next day we enjoyed a day of leisure at Fisherman's Wharf and explored the Bay Area, had dinner at a famous seafood restaurant, shopped in the boutiques and quaint shops along the boardwalk, and retired early, knowing the long trip home would begin the next day.

After breakfast, we repacked the van tightly, anticipating the influx of luggage six people would have, filled the van with gas, had the oil changed, checked the air pressure in the tires and headed to the airport. We were ready.

We were not ready! By the time we added six people and all their belongings to us and ours in the van, we were loaded to the gills, including luggage strapped to the built-in luggage racks on top of the van. We looked like the Clampetts moving to Beverly Hills! And there was little or no wiggle room inside the van with every seat occupied.

With the hatches battened down, though, we finally lumbered across the San Francisco–Oakland Bay Bridge and headed east toward Utah, where we planned to overnight in Salt Lake City. It was a long day, but everything went fairly well, and we arrived at our motel late.

It was a long day, but everything went fairly well, and we arrived at our motel late.

Round two began the next morning early with breakfast and repacking the van with all the paraphernalia we had dislodged the night before. Loren climbed up the ladder on the back of the van to secure the luggage on top, or so I thought. However, without my knowing, he decided that the two largest suitcases were so heavy that they would ride just fine without being strapped down, so he left them unsecured.

From Salt Lake City, we headed southeast to Denver, Colorado. Then we would turn due east into Kansas. As we got into the Rockies and began twisting and turning through the mountains, the winds that naturally whistle through the mountainous areas began to pick up. And by this time, Loren had begun driving . . . like Mario Andretti . . . around the hairpin curves and up and down the majestic hills.

As we came over a particularly steep hill and started down the other side, suddenly the youngest daughter, Kim, yelled, "Hey, Dad, look!"

We all glanced back to see the two large suitcases fly off the roof of the van, bounce into the middle of the two-lane highway, explode open, and fling their silky contents to the wind and all over the road. Yikes!

Loren immediately maneuvered the van to an emergency stop about a hundred yards from the renegade luggage and then backed carefully along the shoulder of the road to where the items were scattered. Making the kids stay in the car, the four adults jumped out of the van and began gathering up clothes, shoes, and multicolored underwear from along the center stripe of the highway and shoving them back into the two now-broken suitcases.

I was doing my lingerie rescue on the other side of the

center stripe when I was startled by screeching tires and the deafening blare of an air horn. Jerking around, I looked up to see a massive eighteen-wheeler truck bearing down on me from the top of the hill. Turning to run, I found myself face to face with an oncoming car in the other lane. So I whirled around and raced back behind the van, just in time to see the truck grind to a stop within a few feet of the two suitcases still lying open in the roadway and the car go flying by on the other side.

I was breathing hard with relief, and the truck driver was shaking his head and wiping sweat from his eyes as he stayed stopped long enough for us to finish our clothing detail. Then he quickly put his big rig in gear and drove away for fear that another vehicle would come over the hill and not be able to stop. We waved in gratitude as he pulled away.

Meanwhile, we repacked the two damaged suitcases, tied them shut with some bungee cords, and this time, guess what? Loren strapped them securely to the luggage racks. Finally, our discombobulated crew climbed back into the van and continued our trek through the mountains, albeit a little more slowly this time.

As little Laura Ingalls often said on *Little House on the Prairie*, "If I had a remembrance book," I would title this adventure "The Great Underwear Escapade." (Eat your heart out, Victoria's Secret!)

Mary Hollingsworth

"If that's your budget, I can sell you this tape. It's the theme song from 'Hawaii Five-O'."

"May I have some stationery?" a man asked the hotel clerk.

"Are you a guest of the hotel?" asked the clerk.

"No, I'm paying eighty dollars a day," said the man.

Tal Bonham

A tourist was vacationing on the sunny and hot Mediterranean island of Malta. He was appalled by the chaotic traffic. Cars and buses were darting every which way with no apparent order. The tourist asked his hotel-keeper why it was so disorderly.

"Well," the hotelkeeper replied, "in some countries they

drive on the right side of the road; in others they drive on the left. Here, we drive in the shade."

Author Unknown

IF I HAD MY LIFE TO LIVE OVER AGAIN

If I had my life to live over again, I'd try to make more mistakes next time.

I would relax, I would limber up, I would be sillier than I have been this trip.

I know of very few things I would take seriously. I would take more trips.

I would be crazier. I would climb more mountains, swim more rivers and watch more sunsets.

I would do more walking and looking. I would eat more ice cream and fewer beans.

I would have more actual troubles, and fewer imaginary ones.

You see, I'm one of those people who live life prophylactically and sensibly hour after hour, day after day. Oh, I've had my moments, and if I had to do it over again I'd have more of them.

In fact, I'd try to have nothing else, just moments, one after another, instead of living so many years ahead each day.

I've been one of those people who never go anywhere without a thermometer, a hot-water bottle, a gargle, a raincoat, aspirin and a parachute.

If I had to do it over again I would go places, do things and travel lighter than I have.

If I had my life to live over, I would start barefooted earlier in the spring and stay that way later in the fall.

I would play hooky more. I wouldn't make such good grades, except by accident.

I would ride on merry-go-rounds. I'd pick more daisies.

Tim Hansel

No one realizes how beautiful it is to travel until he comes home and rests his head on his old, familiar pillow.

Lin Yutang

5

Jest Patriotic

Card-carrying, flag-waving, red-white-and-blue-blooded Americans are proud of it. We love flag ceremonies, fireworks, parades, bands and the Fourth of July. We cry when "The Star-Spangled Banner" is played, and we support our troops, no matter what the war is. And sometimes we laugh at good old US hilarity.

WHAT DO YOU SEE?

The company commander and the first sergeant were in the field for maneuvers. As they hit the sack for the night, the first sergeant said: "Sir, look up into the sky and tell me what you see."

"I see millions of stars," the commander replied.

The first sergeant asked, "What does that tell you, sir?"

The commander answered, "Astronomically, it tells me that there are millions of galaxies and potentially billions of planets. Theologically, it tells me that God is great and that we are small and insignificant. Meteorologically, it tells me that we will have a beautiful day tomorrow. What does it tell you, Top?"

The first sergeant said, "Well, sir, it tells me that somebody stole our tent."

Author Unknown

A soldier in the Civil War who wanted to play it safely put on the coat of a Northern soldier—a blue coat—and the pants of a Southern soldier—gray pants—and tiptoed onto the battlefield. He got shot by both sides.

Leroy Brownlow

As Taft took the stage to address a campaign audience, a band of Roosevelt supporters showered the stage with cabbages. Taft's own supporters grew angry. Sensing trouble, Taft told them all, "Never mind, my friends, our opponents have simply lost their heads."

Michael L. Bromley

TO HONOR A VETERAN

Several years ago my father was killed in a tractor accident in Arkansas. He didn't have much experience on a tractor. He was a military man. He'd seen combat duty in World War II, Korea and Vietnam. For twenty-seven years he'd worn the uniform of his country, and it was decorated with a silver star, a bronze star, and a purple heart. He was to be buried with full military honors at the National Cemetery in Arlington, Virginia. Things like that don't seem to matter to most folks these days.

The lot had fallen to my older brother to drive to Pine Bluff, Arkansas, to pick up the cremated remains of my father and return them to the family home for a memorial service. My brother drove home on Interstate 30 with a plastic box containing my father's remains and an American flag riding on the passenger seat of his pickup. As he drove along, somewhere in east Texas, his emotions started to get the best of him, so he pulled on to the shoulder of the road to cry for a while. He placed the plastic box and the neatly folded flag on the hood of his truck, sat on the bumper and let the tears flow.

It wasn't long before a trucker stopped to see if he was all right. My brother told him the story and showed him the flag. The trucker listened patiently, patted my brother on the shoulder, and said, "Son, it's going to be all right."

The trucker disappeared for a minute and was soon back at my brother's side. In a few minutes, another trucker stopped to pay his respects and to listen to the story of my father's life and passing. A few minutes later, two more truckers stopped to lend their support. Within fifteen minutes, there were more than thirty rigs parked along the interstate. The truckers stood in a semicircle around my father's remains and quietly paid their respects.

One of the truckers took off his cap and said, "Let's have a prayer."

All of the other truckers took off their caps and bowed their heads as a prayer was spoken. After the prayer, each of the truckers had a word of encouragement or strength.

One of the truckers said, "Come on, friend. Follow us into town."

The truckers all turned on their lights and escorted my brother the rest of the way into the Metroplex.

I owe a debt to those unknown truckers. Those men stopped to help what they thought might be a stranded traveler. Instead, they paid a deep honor to a man who had done his duty. Those truckers understood duty, honor and sacrifice. And their kindness helped my family to deal with its grief over the loss of our father.

Bill Paxton

When my brother, Frank, went off to the US Air Force, he was in for a few surprises . . . like underwear. In his first letter home, he described service underwear choices as "big, huge, and good grief!"

Mary Hollingsworth

A DAY FOR HEROES

I leaned against an oak at the side of the road, wishing I were invisible, keeping my distance from my parents on their lawn chairs and my younger siblings scampering about. I hoped none of my friends saw me there. God forbid they caught me waving one of the small American flags Mom bought at Ben Franklin's for a dime. At sixteen, I was too old and definitely too cool for our small town's Memorial Day parade. I ought to be at the lake, I brooded. But, no, the all-day festivities were mandatory in my family.

A high school band marched by, the girl in sequins missing her baton as it tumbled from the sky. Firemen blasted sirens in their polished red trucks. The uniforms on the troop of World War II veterans looked too snug on more than one member.

"Here comes Mema," my father shouted.

Five black convertibles lumbered down the boulevard. The mayor was in the first, handing out programs. I didn't need to look at one. I knew my Uncle Bud's name was printed on it, as it had been every year since he was killed in Italy— our family's war hero. And I knew that, perched on the backseat of one of the cars, waving and smiling, was Mema, my grandmother. She had a corsage on her lapel and a sign in gold embossed letters on the car door: "Gold Star Mother."

I hid behind the tree so I wouldn't have to meet her

gaze. It wasn't because I didn't love her or appreciate her. She'd taught me how to sew, to call a strike in baseball. She made great cinnamon rolls, which we always ate after the parade. What embarrassed me was all the attention she got for a son who had died twenty years earlier. With four other children and a dozen grandchildren, why linger on this one long-ago loss?

I peeked out from behind the oak just in time to see Mema wave and blow my family a kiss as the motorcade moved on. The purple ribbon on her hat fluttered in the breeze.

The rest of our Memorial Day ritual was equally scripted. No use trying to get out of it. I followed my family back to Mema's house, where there was the usual baseball game in the backyard and the same old reminiscing about Uncle Bud in the kitchen. Helping myself to a cinnamon roll, I retreated to the living room and plopped down on an armchair. There I found myself staring at the Army photo on the bookcase of Bud, the uncle I'd never known. I must have looked at him a thousand times—so proud in his crested cap and knotted tie. His uniform was decorated with military emblems that I could never decode. Funny, he was starting to look younger to me as I got older. *Who were you, Uncle Bud?* I nearly asked out loud.

I picked up the photo and turned it over. Yellowing tape held a prayer card that read: "Lloyd 'Bud' Heitzman, 1925–1944. A Great Hero." Nineteen years old when he died, not much older than I was. But a great hero? How could you be a hero at nineteen?

The floorboards creaked behind me. I turned to see Mema coming in from the kitchen, wiping her hands on her apron. I almost hid the photo because I didn't want to listen to the same stories I'd heard year after year: "Your Uncle Bud had this little rat-terrier named Jiggs. Good old Jiggs. How he loved that mutt! He wouldn't go anywhere without Jiggs. He used to put him in the rumble seat of his Chevy coupe and drive all over town. Remember how hard Bud worked after we lost the farm? At haying season, he worked all day, sunrise to sunset, baling for other farmers. Then he brought me all his wages. He'd say, "Mama, someday I'm going to buy you a brand-new farm. I promise." There wasn't a better boy in the world!

Sometimes I wondered about that boy dying alone in a muddy ditch in a foreign country he'd only read about. I thought of the scared kid who jumped out of a foxhole in front of an advancing enemy, only to be downed by a sniper. I couldn't reconcile the image of the boy and his dog with that of the stalwart soldier.

Mema stood beside me for a while, looking at the photo. From outside came the sharp snap of an American flag flapping in the breeze and the voices of my cousins cheering my brother at bat. "Mema," I asked, "what's a hero?" Without a word, she turned and walked down the hall to the back bedroom. I followed.

She opened a bureau drawer and took out a small metal box, then sank down onto the bed.

"These are Bud's things," she said. "They sent them to

us after he died." She opened the lid and handed me a telegram dated October 13, 1944. "The Secretary of War regrets to inform you that your son, Lloyd Heitzman, was killed in Italy." Your son! I imagined Mema reading that sentence for the first time. I didn't know what I would have done if I'd gotten a telegram like that.

"Here's Bud's wallet," she continued. Even after all those years, it was caked with dried mud. Inside was Bud's driver's license with the date of his sixteenth birthday. I compared it with the driver's license I had just received. A photo of Bud holding a little spotted dog fell out of the wallet. Jiggs. Bud looked so pleased with his mutt.

There were other photos in the wallet: a laughing Bud standing arm in arm with two buddies, photos of my mom and aunt and uncle, another of Mema waving. This was the home Uncle Bud took with him, I thought. I could see him in a foxhole, taking out these snapshots to remind himself of how much he was loved and missed.

How heartbreaking to have a life, plans and hopes for the future so brutally snuffed out.

"Who's this?" I asked, pointing to a shot of a pretty dark-haired girl.

"Marie. Bud dated her in high school. He wanted to marry her when he came home." A girlfriend? Marriage? How heartbreaking to have a life, plans and hopes for the future so brutally snuffed out.

Sitting on the bed, Mema and I sifted through the treasures in the box: a gold watch that had never been wound again, a sympathy letter from President Roosevelt and one from Bud's commander, and a medal shaped like a heart, trimmed with a purple ribbon. And at the very bottom, the deed to Mema's house.

"Why's this here?" I asked.

"Because Bud bought this house for me." She explained how, after his death, the US government had given her ten thousand dollars and, with it, she built the house she was still living in.

"He kept his promise all right," Mema said in a quiet voice I'd never heard before.

For a long while, the two of us sat there on the bed. Then we put the wallet, the medal, the letters, the watch, the photos and the deed back into the metal box. I finally understood why it was so important for Mema—and me— to remember Uncle Bud on this day. If he'd lived longer, he might have built that house for Mema or married his high-school girlfriend. There might have been children and grandchildren to remember him by. As it was, there was only that box, the name in the program, and the reminiscing around the kitchen table.

"I guess he was a hero because he gave everything for what he believed," I said carefully.

"Yes, child," Mema replied, wiping a tear with the back of her hand. "Don't ever forget that."

I haven't. Even today with Mema gone, my husband and I take our lawn chairs to the tree-shaded boulevard on Memorial Day and give our three daughters small American flags that I buy for a quarter at Ben Franklin's. I want them to remember that life isn't just about getting what you want. Sometimes it involves giving up the things you love for what you love even more. That a man lay down his life for his friends, was how Christ put it. That many men and women did the same for their country—that's what I think when I see the parade pass by now. And if I close my eyes and imagine, I can still see Mema in her regal purple hat, honoring her son, a true American hero.

Nancy Sullivan Geng

MILITARY COMMON SENSE RULES

A lot of life's problems can be explained by the US military and its applications of common sense:

1. Sometimes I think war is God's way of teaching us geography. (Paul Rodriguez)

2. A slipping gear could let your M203 grenade launcher fire when you least expect it. That would make you quite unpopular in what's left of your unit. (*Army's Magazine of Preventive Maintenance*).

3. Aim towards the enemy. (Instruction printed on US M79 Rocket Launcher)

4. When the pin is pulled, Mr. Grenade is not our friend. (US Marine Corps)

5. Cluster bombing from B-52s is very, very accurate. The bombs always hit the ground. (US Air Force)

6. If the enemy is in range, so are you. (*Infantry Journal*)

7. It is generally inadvisable to eject directly over the area you just bombed. (US Air Force Manual)

8. Whoever said "the pen is mightier than the sword" obviously never encountered automatic weapons. (Gen. Douglas MacArthur)

9. Try to look unimportant; they may be low on ammo. (*Infantry Journal*)

10. You, you, and you . . . panic. The rest of you, come with me. (Marine Gunnery Sergeant)

11. Tracers work both ways. (US Army Ordnance)

12. Five-second fuses only last three seconds. (*Infantry Journal*)

13. Don't ever be the first, don't ever be the last, and don't ever volunteer to do anything. (US Navy Seaman)

14. Bravery is being the only one who knows you're afraid. (David Hackworth)

15. If your attack is going too well, you have walked into an ambush. (*Infantry Journal*)

16. No combat-ready unit has ever passed inspection. (Joe Gay)

17. Any ship can be a minesweeper . . . once. (Admiral Hornblower)

18. Never tell the Platoon Sergeant you have nothing to do. (Unknown Marine Recruit)

19. Don't draw fire; it irritates the people around you. (Your Buddies)

20. Mines are equal opportunity weapons. (Army Platoon Sergeant)

21. If you find yourself in a fair fight, you didn't plan your mission properly. (David Hackworth)

22. In the Navy, the Chief is always right. (Written on the Door into the Chief's Quarters)

Author Unknown

TRADING UP

One stormy night, a Marine private was on his first guard-duty assignment.

Presently, a general stepped out to take his dog for a walk.

The nervous young private snapped to attention, made a perfect salute, and cried out, "Sir, good evening, sir!"

The general, out for some relaxation, returned the salute and said, "Good evening, soldier. Nice night, isn't it?"

It was hardly a nice night, but the private wasn't about to disagree with the general, so he saluted again and replied, "Sir, yes, sir!"

The general continued, "You know there's something

about a stormy night that I find soothing. It's all really relaxing, don't you agree?"

The private didn't agree, but then the private was just a private, and responded, "Sir, yes, sir!"

Indicating the dog, the general said, "This is a Golden Retriever, the best type of dog to train."

The private glanced at the dog and saluted yet again. "Sir, yes, sir!"

The general continued, "I got this dog for my wife!"

The private said, "Good trade, sir!"

Author Unknown

THE STORY OF "TAPS"

O f all the bugle calls used in the United States armed services, none is more popular or better known than "Taps." Probably not one American in twenty has heard of how this famous call was first blown.

It happened in Virginia in July 1862. After seven days of bitter fighting before Richmond, the North's Army of the Potomac lay encamped at Harrison's Landing on the James River. Vacant places in the ranks were a sharp reminder of the heavy losses that had been suffered, and to officers and men alike, there now came a sobering realization of what a terrible toll the War Between the States was sure to take before it was over.

Up and down the long, winding valley rose the bugle

calls, echoing to the distant hills. The rhythm of camp life was punctuated by these soaring notes. If it had not been for tents and uniforms, the setting would have suited a summer idyll.

Now, with time heavy on his hands, the thoughts of more than one soldier turned to home and loved ones in the North. As nostalgia rested heavily on the troops, the close of each day found many men in a mood not untouched with sadness.

Some of this feeling must have crept into the consciousness of Gen. Daniel Butterfield. A brave commander, he was also an expert musician, with ears keenly attuned to harmony. While homesickness pervaded the Army and the nights were filled with tender retrospection, he took a sudden dislike to the discordant "Lights Out" call, which had been handed down from the early days of West Point.

All by himself, he began to turn over in his mind a combination of notes that would express the peacefulness of a great camp after nightfall—soldiers sleeping, sentries keeping watch under the stars, rest after labor. The scene must have inspired the musical phrases of "Taps."

When General Butterfield was satisfied with his musical combination, he sent for his brigade bugler, Oliver W. Norton. Whistling the notes over and over, he taught them to the young musician. Whenever Norton made a mistake, General Butterfield would correct him, and the result was that in a short time the bugler was able to blow "Taps" perfectly. In order to preserve the call, the general copied down the notes with a pencil on the back of an old envelope.

That same night General Butterfield's brigade was the first to hear the lingering refrain. Its music carried up and down the valley, and the wistful, haunting notes struck a responsive chord with thousands of other listeners.

The next morning General Butterfield was besieged by the buglers of other camps. "Taps" had caught their fancy, and they were curious about it. They wanted to know its origin and its meaning, and even asked for a copy of the music. All were given permission to use it.

Whenever the new "Lights Out" was blown among Union forces after that, it excited immediate interest. The music lingered in the memory, and every soldier came to love it. It passed from corps to corps until, at last, by general orders, it was substituted for the old "Lights Out" call and was officially printed in the army regulations.

Since that time, as everybody knows, "Taps" has become an American tradition. It is used for the military burial service by the veterans of all wars. That use has undoubtedly given it the most poignant associations. It moves listeners as no other bugle call can, and at the first notes a hush will fall over the noisiest crowd.

"Taps"...moves listeners as no other bugle call can...

Life was certainly kind to the call's composer. At the close of the war, General Butterfield entered business in New York, where, by reason of his great organizing ability, he was frequently called upon to take charge of public parades and exhibitions. When he finally retired, it was to a home at Cold Spring, New York, where, just across the Hudson, he could hear the notes of his beloved "Taps" sounded every evening by the bugler at West Point.

George Daniels

THE TOP 9 PENTAGON PROJECT ICE CREAM NAMES

9.   A Thousand Points of Mint

8.   Nukies and Cream

7. $800 Wrench Ripple

6.   Taxation Sensation

5.   Blowings' Mocha

4.   Taxpayer Crunched

3.   Defense Contractors' Delight

2.   Delicious Fictitious Budget Crunch

1.   Budget Fudge-It

Ben Cohen

FORCED LANDING

The student in his primary trainer was flying a solo cross-country. He lost his way and before he finally ran out of fuel he decided to put it down on a road. With hardly any cars on the road, he managed to coast his aircraft into a gas station and said to the attendant, "Fill 'er up!"

The attendant just looked at the pilot.

"I bet you don't get too many airplanes asking for a refuel," said the pilot.

The attendant replied: "True, most pilots use that airport over there."

Martin Leeuwis

THIS LITTLE CANDLE OF MINE

Blackouts can be frightening (unless they happen during dinner at my house, and you can't see what you're eating).

The town I live in tends to be a bit windy at times, and the wind sometimes triggers power failures. This is exactly what happened one night while my family and I were on the twenty-eighth minute of *60 Minutes*.

"Is it dark in here to the rest of you, or did I just go blind?" I asked, cautiously maneuvering my way to the light switch.

"It's another blackout," my husband's voice echoed through the darkness.

I flicked the switch, but nothing happened.

"It must be the wind again," he said.

"How hard is it blowing?"

"Its usual," he replied as an uprooted eucalyptus tree flew by the window. "We'd better get out the candles. Any idea where they are?"

"The same place they were during the last blackout," I answered.

"Where's that?"

"Wal-Mart. We never bought any."

"Well," he said, "there must be something around here that we could roll up and use as a torch."

I handed him a stack of our bills.

"Sweetheart," he said, "we only need a two-hour torch, not the eternal flame!"

Luckily, for our creditors at least, the silhouette of one of our sons appeared in the doorway, holding what appeared to be the remains of an old birthday candle.

"Perfect!" my husband exclaimed a he grabbed the splinter of wax and quickly lit it.

After looking around for something to set it in (we finally settled on a Twinkie), I began to realize what it must have been like for our forefathers. They had to do everything without electricity. They didn't have light bulbs, fax machines, video games or VCRs. They had to rough it, and they survived.

About that time, though, the power came back on and everyone resumed watching television. Everyone but me, that is.

As I watched our little candle flickering vainly beneath the fluorescent lights, I could feel that pioneer spirit welling up inside me. I thought to myself, *Who needs progress? We could live just like our ancestors, without modern conveniences and astronomical utility bills.*

I quickly surveyed all the electric gadgets in our home. For lighting, we could use kerosene lamps. Instead of watching television, we could read . . . what were those things called? Oh yeah, books. As for the washing machine, I could go to the river and beat our clothes against a rock. (If I accidentally ripped them in the knees, they'd be in style anyway.) I was absolutely convinced we could make it without the comforts of modern technology.

But when I glanced over at my microwave, I knew I had to reassess my plan. My microwave and I were old friends. I couldn't imagine life without it. I couldn't go back to those days of toiling and sweating in a drive-thru lane for dinner.

I thought for a moment of those pre-Swanson, pre-Lean Cuisine years, then did the only thing a self-respecting American could do—I blew out the candle and ate the Twinkie.

Martha Bolton

ONLY IN AMERICA...

Can a pizza get to your house faster than an ambulance;

Are there handicapped parking places in front of a skating rink;

Do people order double cheeseburgers, large fries and a diet soda;

Do banks leave both doors open and then chain the pens to the counters;

Do we leave cars worth thousands of dollars in the driveway and leave useless junk in boxes in the garage;

Do we use answering machines to screen calls and then have call waiting so we won't miss a call from someone we didn't want to talk to in the first place;

Do we buy hot dogs in packages of ten and buns in packages of eight;

Do we use the word politics to accurately describe the process: Poli in Latin means "many" and tics are "blood-sucking creatures."

Jim Kraus

MORE! MORE!

Lt. Gitz Rice was a member of a famous Canadian regiment that went to France in World War I. The regiment fought in Flanders Fields. It fought across the desolate "No Man's Land" under cover of a fearsome barrage, sometimes even without the protection of the sheltering shells.

Rice's company carried a strange implement of war with them—an old dilapidated piano. On that old piano in France, Gitz Rice composed one of the famous songs of the soldiers, "Mademoiselle from Armentieres."

The afternoon before Christmas Eve, the Canadians decided that the piano should be taken up to the front-line trenches. It was hoisted into an army truck and finally deposited at its destination.

Forced peace had settled over "No Man's Land" that night, but the barbed wire remained, and a morning attack threatened each side. The hostile troops were so close that the Canadian soldiers could hear the Germans talking to each other.

Shortly before the hour of midnight, Rice began playing Christmas carols in the British trench. First, he played "Silent Night, Holy Night." This was followed by "Hark! The Herald Angels Sing" and other beloved carols familiar to all the Christian world.

The Canadian soldiers sang quietly at first and then lustily. Then they paused, thinking they were hearing an echo from the surrounding hills. From across the shallow field, they heard the German troops singing with them. It was Christmas Eve.

Rice then played an aria from Wagner's "Tannhäuser." As he began the opening chords, a Canadian soldier mounted the rim of the parapet and, in plain sight of the Germans, sang the words of the aria.

When the aria stopped, silence fell over the field. Then, suddenly, a cry broke out from the Germans: "More! More!" So one of their own singers, a rich baritone, repeated the song to Rice's accompaniment, standing silhouetted against the moonlight as a clear target for British rifles. And when he finished, the Canadians cheered and cried out, "More! More!"

No rifle fire was heard that Christmas Eve. No singer was shot.

Hatred had, at least for that one heaven-touched night, melted into love in memory of One greater than any war or enemy. And when I look around at the hatred, distrust, and prejudice that poison our world today, I want to cry out for everyone to hear, "More! More!" More love. More hope. More peace. More of the One who is greater than any war or enemy.

From World War I Records

President Calvin Coolidge once entertained some friends from Vermont in the White House. His friends were concerned that they display proper table manners to win the President's respect, so they observed Coolidge very carefully and followed his example in detail. The meal passed smoothly. Then coffee was served. Coolidge poured his into his saucer. The guests did likewise. Then Coolidge added sugar and cream. The visitors did the same. Coolidge then leaned over and gave his coffee to the cat.

Henry Charles Sutter

SO LONG AS THERE ARE HOMES

So long as there are homes to which men turn

At the close of day,

So long as there are homes where children are—

Where women stay,

If love and loyalty and faith be found

Across these sills,

A stricken nation can recover from

Its gravest ills.

So long as there are homes where fires burn

And there is bread,

So long as there are homes where lamps are lit

And prayers are said;

Although a people falters through the dark

And nations grope,

With God Himself back of these little homes

We still can hope.

Grace Nell Crowell

CAROLYN TO TOWER

Carolyn was so excited she could hardly stand it. Today, the officers' wives of the new flight class at the Ft. Rucker, Alabama, US Army flight school were going to be treated to a grand tour of the facility and the aircraft. Best of all, each wife would be allowed to sit in the airplanes and helicopters their husbands were learning to fly.

Sure enough, the women were treated like royalty, escorted everywhere by uniformed officers and wined and dined in the Officers' Club. Following lunch, the moment came that Carolyn had long awaited. She would be allowed to climb into the Beaver airplane that her husband had been raving about every night.

A young aviator handed her up to the cockpit, and she sat there pretending she was the flyer. *Zooom, zoooom*, she hummed to herself. This experience was the best yet. She looked out the window and saw her husband give her a little thumbs up as she had the time of her life.

Then she spotted the radio mike—or at least what she assumed was the microphone. She pulled it to her mouth and said, "Carolyn to tower. Lieutenant Carolyn to tower."

Loving her pretend game, she pressed her mouth even further into the tube and again intoned, "Carolyn to tower. Ready for takeoff."

This was so much fun that Carolyn didn't want to leave the airplane when the soldier offered his hand. She wondered why he was smothering a smile. She wondered even more when she looked over to where her husband stood with his class. He was red-faced and seemed to be choking, as did the rest of his classmates. Curious, she walked up to him and asked what all the giggling was about.

Finally breaking into a full-blown laugh, he informed her, "Honey, that tube you were speaking into like a microphone wasn't what you thought it was. It was a urinal, a relief tube the pilots use when they have to go to the bathroom!"

Vicki P. Graham

"Oh, you won't do me any harm, sir — the Government destroyed my incentive *years* ago!"

I was just wondering . . . we're being bombarded with terrorism, tornadoes, hurricanes, war, pornography, political scandals, murder and mayhem (not to mention that Texas needs rain). Do we really think it's a wise move to take God out of the Pledge of Allegiance and remove Christ from Christmas?

Mary Hollingsworth

OVERRATED

On his way to a reception held in his honor, Grant, caught in a rain shower, offered the shelter of his umbrella to a stranger walking in the same direction as he. The stranger was also bound for the reception, but confided that he was going only to satisfy a personal curiosity, having never seen Grant. "Between us, I have always thought that Grant was a very much overrated man," he explained. "That's my view also," Grant said.

Horace Greene

MY OTHER DADDY

During the scary days of the Bay of Pigs incident, my brother-in-law Loren Hollingsworth was a Green Beret in the US Marines. He was on high alert, expecting to be called up for duty at any moment. When the call came, he did exactly what he had always done in preparation for a mission—he packed his military gear, pressed his uniforms, got a military haircut and shaved off his mustache and beard, which he otherwise kept.

Not realizing the effect this would have on his baby daughter, Julie, he was surprised when she would no longer have anything to do with him. She didn't recognize him without his beard and mustache. And she kept asking, "Where's my daddy?"

"Boy, that'll take the wind right out of your sails," said Loren when telling me the story.

Loren left on the mission and was gone for a few weeks. When he returned home, even though my sister-in-law, Penny, had been trying to help their little girl through the hairless-dad issue, Julie didn't recognize him and wouldn't have much to do with him for a long time.

One day he had taken her into the backyard and was pushing her gently in her swing. They were laughing and playing, having a wonderful time. Suddenly, little Julie looked at Loren seriously and said, "You're nice . . . but you're not like my other daddy."

The price of patriotism!

Mary Hollingsworth

A DAY TO REMEMBER

The following story was written by Guideposts founder Norman Vincent Peale upon the return of troops from Vietnam in the 1970s. Its message is just as true for America now as it was then.

When I was a small boy in a sleepy American town, we looked forward all year to the Fourth of July: flags snapping in the wind, trombones glinting and blaring, red white and blue bunting on the speaker's platform, the gleeful stutter of firecrackers, the hot sunshine, the gentle sky and— over everything—a wonderful soaring sense of pride and patriotism and belonging. "The glorious Fourth," old-timers still called it, because that's what it was.

But how long is it since we had one? Quite a while, wouldn't you say? Somehow as the years went by, the American dream faltered and a certain cynicism crept in. Flag-waving became a term of reproach. Gradually, our country's birthday became just another tepid holiday marked by grim traffic statistics and discarded beer cans.

This year—I truly believe—things are going to be

different, and the reason is simple. As I write these words, a bitter conflict has ended, and our prisoners of war are coming home. It is the return of these splendid men with all their courage and dignity and endurance that has rekindled the dormant spark, the banked fires of patriotism in our hearts.

There was a certain six-year-old who stood among the welcomers as our men came off the plane that brought them back from captivity. Caught up in the surging emotions of the crowd, he looked at his mother with shining eyes.

"When I grow up," he whispered, "can I be like them?" With the insight often granted to children, that little boy knew that it was not enough to applaud, to admire—not even enough to be grateful. Something told him that he stood in the presence of human qualities so completely admirable that they deserved to be studied, copied, absorbed into our own personalities and lives.

Can this be done? I think it can. In fact, one way to enhance the Fourth of July this year would be to spend a small part of the day thinking about these men, remembering what they suffered and what it was that brought them so triumphantly through their ordeal. None of us, thank God, has to face what they went through.

Most of us, however, have lesser problems and burdens. Isn't it conceivable that, if we think deeply enough and remember strongly enough, some of the attitudes that sustained them through their years of trial might also support and strengthen us?

What were those attitudes? It seems to me there were three. First—and they stressed this above all—was the belief that a loving and compassionate God exists, that He cares about human suffering, and that He will give strength and courage to those who call on Him. Most of us believe in such a God, but too often we take Him for granted. We don't turn to Him because our problems aren't big enough. We think we can handle them ourselves.

> Our prisoners of war had no such illusions. They knew they couldn't make it on their own.

Our prisoners of war had no such illusions. They knew they couldn't make it on their own. They had to seek enormous power to cope with enormous difficulties. And they found it.

Faith—rocklike, unassailable, unshakable. These men found it. It sustained them. Perhaps we can strengthen ours by remembering theirs.

The second thing they had was discipline. Not just military discipline (they had that too), but tremendous inner-directed control over their minds and bodies. They knew that their greatest enemies were not their captors but the inertia, monotony and hopelessness that lead to despair.

They fought these invisible adversaries in every way possible—with strenuous physical exercise, with disciplined mental endeavors—they wrote down biblical passages from memory; they compiled crude textbooks of French and Spanish phrases; one man laboriously put together a 312-page English grammar book. Another laboriously stitched together an American flag from pieces of blanket, underwear and towels. It was flown at night in the Hanoi Hilton cellblock.

They forced themselves to communicate—describing past experiences, inventing stories, recalling the plots of movies they had once seen. They even disciplined their fantasies—in his mind, one captive designed and built the home he had always wanted, room by room, brick by brick.

Discipline—what is it anyway? It's the capacity to endure the unwelcome in order to achieve the desirable, isn't it? Few of us have enough of it in our lives. But if we think about those men, a little more of it may come to us.

The third thing they had was a remarkable kind of outflowing love. They had it for one another. For many, their favorite greeting, even to a professed agnostic or atheist, was "God bless you." This could not have been an empty phrase; it must have been a heartfelt prayer. They felt this love for their country with the kind of longing that only those who have been deprived of something priceless can truly know. They felt it for their wives, for their children, for their friends, for freedom, for life itself. It enveloped them as they came off the planes that brought them home, in a glow of warmth and joy that illuminated everything.

It was in the face of a black sergeant weeping on the shoulder of a white Marine captain as the band played "America the Beautiful." It was in the flying footsteps as wives flung themselves into arms that had been empty for so long. It was in the solemn handshake of the seven-year-old who had never before seen his father. It was in the ecstatic hugs of those who did remember. "There's something great," said Navy Capt. James A. Mulligan, "about kids waving American flags." Exactly so.

Will such things fade and be forgotten? Perhaps in the end they will. But not just yet. Not this year, anyway. They are still here with us, close enough to draw strength from, close enough to reach out and touch—especially on July Fourth, the day that has meant so much to Americans ever since this nation was founded. Once more we can have a glorious Fourth—if we will just remember.

Norman Vincent Peale

I don't make jokes; I just watch the government and report the facts.
Will Rogers

I'm desperately trying to figure out why kamikaze pilots wore helmets.
Dave Edison

MY NAME IS AMERICA

I am a country . . .

But I am more than a country. I am over two hundred years old, but my mountains, forests and rivers are ageless. Before I was a dream in the minds of mortal men, the land was a beautiful reality in the hands of a beneficent Creator.

I am a nation . . .

But I am more than a nation. I am a republic of fifty sovereign states, each with its own heritage and individual greatness, each a vital part of one indivisible whole—the United States of America.

I am a government . . .

But I am more than a government. I am a symbol of plenty, a model of representative government, a hallmark of freedom, justice and independence to hundred of millions throughout the world.

I am a melting pot . . .

But I am more than a melting pot. I am a haven for the oppressed, a living adventure in brotherhood, a community of compassion, and a dynamic example of liberty under law, opportunity with responsibility, and democracy through equality.

My name is America!

William Arthur Ward

6

Little Wonders

*Kids are light and life itself! They're energy,
enthusiasm, inquisitiveness, ingenuity and
entertainment all rolled up into tiny bodies.
They're sources of hope, faith and definitely
laughter. They make life worth living.*

AND TAKE US TO HEAVEN

John was almost five years old that Christmas Eve. He was filled with awe and curiosity.

Debbie, John's aunt, was visiting during the week before Christmas. She usually stayed away from family during this time of year. Anything that reminded her of family, especially children, hurt too much. But this year her sister, John's mother, asked her to come and see John in his first Christmas play.

No, that wasn't right, she didn't ask me, Debbie thought. *She begged me. She should know more than anyone else how much it hurts to see children this time of year.*

Almost five years ago to the day, Debbie had lost her own son and husband in a freak car accident. They, too, were going to a Christmas pageant. Her husband was the choir director, and her son was going to sing with the little angel chorus. But they didn't make it. A patch of ice, a sudden swerve, a giant oak looming up before them, and her life ended.

No, I didn't die. But I wish I had. Thoughts came flooding back to her and tears welled up in her eyes as she sat in the church pew waiting for the play to begin. She glanced around the building that she had not been in since that night. Debbie had been what most people would have called a strong Christian—always the first to volunteer to take food to the sick, teach Sunday school class, or whatever needed to be done. But her faith wasn't enough to hold her up when her world crumbled.

Oh, well-meaning people had come and visited her the first few weeks after the double funeral, but as time passed, fewer and fewer people came. *Everyone just expected me to forget, to go on as if nothing happened!* Debbie thought angrily.

I've got to get out of here, she thought in panic. *I can't stay here. What was I thinking?* Debbie started to get up and inch her way down an already packed pew when she remembered her sister Chris said that this Christmas held something special for her. With a sigh, she sat back down. Okay, sis, whatever it is that is special for me this year, you had better show it to me, and soon.

John didn't have an important part in the pageant; he

was just one of many in the kindergarten class. As the children gathered for the program, the teachers were busy preparing the costumes of Mary, Joseph, the angels, shepherds and wise men. No one noticed a little boy go out the door into the hall.

But little John had heard a baby crying. There was to be a baby in the pageant—he knew that. But why was it crying?

He wondered why God didn't send the star to guide him. . . .

Down the dark hall he tiptoed. He wondered why God didn't send the star to guide him, and then he remembered: The star wasn't for him. It was for the wise men. He'd have to be very brave and go alone in the dark to find the baby. He turned the corner cautiously.

At the far end of the hall, he saw a light coming from a doorway. Then he heard the baby's cry more clearly. So he crept to the door and peeked in.

Mary Meadowcroft knelt beside the brown beanbag chair her husband had brought as a prop as she put baby Jeffrey down to nap. He was normally a contented baby. The sudden presence of so many eager children frightened Jeffrey, and he had begun crying. *At least the program won't be long*, Mary thought. She decided to wait in the empty classroom with the baby—so his crying would not disturb anyone—until they had to go onstage.

Suddenly, she was startled to hear a little voice questioning, "Are you Mary?"

"Why, yes, I am," she answered with amazement. "Do I know you?"

"I came to see the baby," said John softly, "I didn't know He ever cried like that."

"Jeffrey is just frightened to be in a strange place."

"Hi," John said softly as he knelt down beside the baby. "I'm John. I'm not a wise man or anything, but they couldn't come."

The baby stopped crying to turn and look at John. Mary remained perfectly still, her mouth drawn into an astonished "Oh!"

"I forgot to bring you something, little Jeffrey Jesus."

The baby was smiling now. John put out a tentative finger to touch him and said in whispered adoration, "I really do love you, Jeffrey Jesus."

Suddenly, John smiled. "I know what I can give you! I'll sing you a song that we've been practicing! I know all the words."

Back in the sanctuary, Chris was frantic. The program was about to start, and John was missing. Knowing that her sister, Debbie, was probably talking herself into leaving, she went to get her to help with the search. *That way, if the program doesn't start on time, she has no reason to sneak out,* thought Chris.

Just as they rounded a corner, they heard a small, soft voice, like that of an angel singing. Debbie looked at Chris to see if she heard the same thing. Not wanting to say anything and interrupt the sweet melody, Chris pointed toward a partially opened classroom door. Debbie nodded. They stopped in the doorway at the sight of Mary and the baby, listening to John's quiet gift of song.

Bless all the dear children
In your tender care,
And take us to Heaven
To live with you there.

As little John sang, baby Jeffrey Jesus grasped John's finger in his tiny hand and drifted off to sleep. And Debbie, her eyes glistening with sudden tears, glimpsed a tiny angel that night—an angel that was safe and happy in heaven. *Chris was right,* thought Debbie. This Christmas did bring me something very special—peace.

Rhonda Hogan

Oh! If only we could learn to "love past" things as children do—wrinkles, warts, handicaps, skin colors, blunderings, cultural differences, a grandparent's funny underwear and even meanness. Then the world would be a fit place to live.

Mary Hollingsworth

During the "children's sermon," the minister was talking about Communion and what it is all about.

"The Bible talks of Holy Communion being a 'joyful feast.' What does that mean? Well, 'joyful' means happy, right? And a feast is a meal. So a 'joyful feast' is a happy meal. He paused. And what are the three things we need for a happy meal?"

A little boy put up his hand and said, "Hamburger, fries and a regular soft drink?"

J. John and Mark Stibbe

THE FAMILY CIRCUS　　　**By Bill Keane**

"...and last but not least, Dear Lord, take care of yourself. If you don't, we're all in trouble."

"KIDS WHO ARE DIFFERENT"

Here's to the kids who are different,

Kids who don't always get A's,

Kids who have ears

Twice the size of their peers',

And noses that go on for days.

Here's to the kids who are different,

Kids they call stupid or dumb,

Kids who don't fit,

With the guts and the grit

To dance to a different drum.

Here's to the kids who are different,

Kids with that mischievous streak,

For when they have grown,

As history has shown,

It's the difference that makes them unique.

Digby Wolfe

SIMPLE GESTURES BLOSSOM

Leah was surprised when our son, Josh, presented her with a single violet in a little clay pot on Mother's Day. She had decided not to send him to kindergarten with money for the flower sale, since every penny counted in those days. Josh smiled proudly. "Happy Mother's Day!"

Leah later learned that a kind teacher had given Josh some change for the gift. "He was going to spend his milk money on it," the teacher told her. "I knew you wouldn't want him to do that."

Every morning Leah looked at that little clay pot and smiled. In June, she and Josh took the single violet outside and planted it in the front yard. We watered it all summer and missed it in the winter. Come spring, the little violet returned—this time bringing dozens more. A year later those dozens turned into a hundred.

Thirty years later, Josh is a grown man, our finances are secure and our front yard is filled with violets. Thousands of them. They have never spread into the field behind the house or into any of the neighbors' yards.

On spring mornings I like to look out at that ocean of violets. All from one little flower in a clay pot, bought for the price of a child's carton of milk. Two gestures of love—from a child to his mother and a teacher to a child—and still, all these years later, the beauty of it remains. Leah says it's the best Mother's Day present she ever got—a living reminder of what love can do.

Paul Brinks

Life is a flame that is always
burning itself out,
but it catches fire again
every time a child is born.

George Bernard Shaw

AND A LITTLE CHILD SHALL MISLEAD THEM

One of our favorite jobs has been leading junior church (motto: "If your kids aren't civilized enough to sit quietly for one hour, send 'em to us!"). Our program embraces kids of almost all ages. Anyone not in a diaper is welcome.

We try to do more than babysit our church's beloved little ankle-biters during their time in our special junior church facility (also known as "the unfinished basement"). We aim to give them a solid background in biblical history. And we hold ourselves accountable. At the end of each year, we give the kids paper and pencils, shoot them with tranquilizer darts, and ask them to chronicle what they have learned. And, of course, we're kidding about shooting our little curtain-monkeys with tranquilizer darts.

This assignment never fails to elicit some intriguing responses. We're amazed at how much we can teach kids about the Bible in only a few short months. In case you're a little foggy on your biblical history, let our junior church students help you with this complete overview of the Bible, compiled from their essays:

In the beginning, which occurred near the start, there was nothing but God, darkness and some gas. The Bible says, "The Lord thy God is one," but I think He must be a lot older than that. Anyway, God said, "Give me a light!" and someone did. Then God made the world. He split the Adam and made Eve. Adam and Eve were naked, but they weren't embarrassed because mirrors hadn't been invented yet. Adam and Eve disobeyed God by eating one bad apple, so they were driven from the Garden of Eden. Not sure what they were driven in though because they didn't have cars. After that, people couldn't live forever and stuff. God said He was just going to let nature take its curse.

Adam and Eve had a son, Cain, who hated his brother as long as he was Abel. Pretty soon, all of the early people died off except for Methuselah, who lived to be like a million or something.

One of the next important people was Noah, who was a good guy, but one of his kids was kind of a ham. Noah built a large boat and put his family and some animals on it. He asked some other people to join him, but they said they would have to take a rain check. Then it poured for forty days and forty nights. Next, Noah sent a dove out to find the Olive Garden and check if it was still under water.

After Noah came Abraham, Isaac and Jacob. Jacob was more famous than his brother, Esau, because Esau sold Jacob his birthmark in exchange for some pot roast. Jacob had a son named Joseph who wore a really loud sports coat. Joseph thought he was going to be a great leader, but his brothers said, "In your dreams, buddy!"

Another important Bible guy is Moses, whose real name was Charlton Heston. Moses led the Israel Lights out of Egypt and away from the evil Pharaoh after God sent ten plagues on Pharaoh's people. These plagues included frogs, mice, lice, bowels and no cable. After God helped the Israel

Lights escape, He fed them every day with manicotti. Then He gave them His top Ten Commandments. These include don't lie, cheat, smoke, dance or covet your neighbor's bottom (the Bible uses a bad word for bottom that I'm not supposed to say. But my dad uses it sometimes when he talks about the President). Anyway, those are pretty much the only commandments I remember. Oh yeah, I just thought of one more: Humor thy father and thy mother.

One of Moses' best helpers was Joshua, who is also my cousin Joshua's name. Anyway, Joshua was the first Bible guy to use spies. He sent them to spy on the enemy, but they almost got caught. Luckily, Rahab the Protestant helped them escape. Then Joshua fought the battle of Geritol and the fence fell over on the town.

After Joshua came David. He got to be king by killing a giant with a slingshot. (But when I use my slingshot on my cat, I always get in trouble. PS: I didn't kill my cat, but I almost put her eye out). But David wasn't all good. He did a bad thing by spying on a woman named Sheba while she was taking a bath. (My mom says I shouldn't bother her while she's taking a bath and that I should just go watch cartoons or something.)

David had a son named Solomon who had about three hundred wives and five hundred porcupines. My teacher says he was wise, but that doesn't sound very wise to me. After Solomon, there were a bunch of major league prophets. One of these was Jonah, who was swallowed by a big whale and then barfed up on the shore. There were also some minor league prophets, but I guess we don't have to worry about them.

After the Old Testament came the New Testament. The New Testament is about two thousand years old, so I'm not sure it should be called "new" anymore. Jesus is the star of the New Testament. He was born in Bethlehem in a barn. (I wish I had been born in a barn, too, because my mom is always saying to me, "Close the door! Were you born in a barn?" It would be nice to say, "As a matter of fact, I was.") Also, Jesus was born on Christmas Day, so I feel a little sorry for Him, having His birthday so close to Christmas and all.

During His life, Jesus had many arguments with sinners like the Pharisees and the Republicans. Jesus also had twelve opossums. The worst one was Judas Asparagus. Judas was so evil that they named a terrible vegetable after him. He later died of apostate cancer.

Jesus was a great man. He healed many leopards and even preached to some Germans on the Mount. But the Republicans and all those guys put Jesus on trial before Pontius the Pilot. Pilot didn't stick up for Jesus. He just washed his hands instead.

Anyway, Jesus died for our sins, then came back to life again. He went up to heaven but will be back at the end of the Aluminum. His return is foretold in the book of Revolution.

Todd and Jedd Hafer

Children need love, especially when they don't
deserve it.

Harold S. Hubert

THE GLORY ON HIGHWAY 69

On the night of December 1, we'll turn on the Christmas lights, the ones that take us three months to put up each year. I hope our married daughter will be able to make it over from Talladega, Alabama, for the lighting. After all, she's the reason for the lights.

Her name is Ruby, same as mine, but when she came along, a girl after three boys, everybody called her "Sis," and the name stuck. Sis was five when she started saying how she wished other people could enjoy our lights. We had just one string then, on the tree in the living room.

"They're so beautiful, Mother! I want everyone to see them!"

That was Sis, always wanting good things for others. Well, the next year we bought a second string and hung them on the bush by the front door, where they glowed warm and cheerful for folks driving by on Highway 69. Sis was beside herself with excitement. "I wish we could put dozens of lights out there!"

Lights cost money, of course, and we've never had a lot

of that. Harold's a cook at a roadside restaurant, and I'm a seamstress at Oneita Mills. Still, Sis enjoyed the lights so much that, each year, we managed to buy a few more. We strung them along the porch and wound them around the fence posts. One year Harold figured out a way to get lights high up in the old oak tree: He tied a length of string to a metal nut and fired it into the tree from a slingshot. When the nut dropped down over a branch, he attached a string of lights to it and hauled it up. Another year he made a frame to hold a star for the roof; we saved up and bought a lighted Nativity scene for the year so people wouldn't miss the reason for the celebration.

After a while, folks started driving by just to see our light display. "Mother!" Sis would call as a car's tires crunched on the driveway. "Here comes another one!"

As years went by, it took more and more time to get those thousands of lights up. Electric bills were bigger, too, to keep the lights burning every night for a month. But we managed fine. So many people started coming that Harold cleared a place for parking behind the house and looped the driveway back out to the road so traffic could move in a circle. Still, some nights the line of cars stretches clear down 69, and folks wait half an hour to get close.

Sis got married after high school and moved to Talladega, ninety miles away. That was twenty years ago, but these are still "Sis's lights," and while we're putting them out in the fall, she comes over whenever she can to help us connect the strings and check for burned-out bulbs.

It takes every night after work and all day weekends to get hundreds of strings up on the roof and around the chicken house and up in the trees by the first day of December, when Harold throws the switch. Then a month later, we start taking them down, wrapping each string separately in a plastic storage bag, storing them in the attic with the Baby Jesus and the sheep and the angels. It's almost the end of February—that's nearly six months—before we're done.

Five years ago I had a heart attack, and now I don't do much climbing and hammering. Nothing slows down Harold, though, and there's lots I can do sitting down: check the wiring, replace bulbs. You can't find the old-timey ones anymore, Sis's favorites, shaped like flowers or Christmas figures. "But I love them all, Mother!" she'll say, fingering the strands of bulbs—the sharp-pointed miniatures, the big flame-shaped ones that can burn your fingers.

You see, Sis's fingers tell her when a bulb's burned out: It's cold. Sis can't actually see the lights, never could. She was born blind. That's why every light we hang is for her. For the little girl who squealed with happiness as I guided her hands along that first string, telling her, "This bulb is red . . . this one is yellow . . ." For the girl who said, "Oh, Mother, they're so beautiful! I want everyone to see them too!"

Ruby Swindle

What did you learn in Sunday school, today?" the mother asked her six-year-old.

"We were studying Adam and Eve, Mama," the little girl replied. "How God made the first man. But the man was lonely and so God made the man fall asleep and while he was snoring away, God took out his brains and made a woman from them for him."

James E. Myers

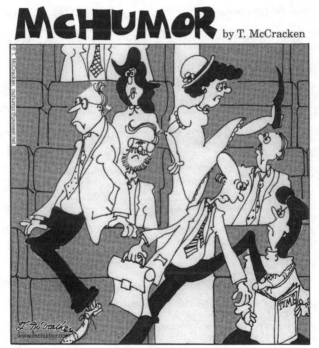

MCHUMOR by T. McCracken

Travel Law #135:
Those with window seats are the last to arrive.

A man finds out what is meant by a spitting image when he tries to feed cereal to his infant.

Imogene Fey

During a dinner party, the hosts' two little children entered the dining room totally nude and walked slowly around the table.

The parents were so embarrassed that they pretended nothing was happening and kept the conversation going.

The guests cooperated and also continued as if nothing extraordinary was happening. After going all the way around the room, the children left.

As they disappeared out of sight, there was a moment of silence at the table, during which one child was heard to say, "You see, it is vanishing cream!"

J. John and Mark Stibbe

You know it's going to be a bad day when your four-year-old announces that it's almost impossible to flush a grapefruit.

Sandra P. Aldrich

Kids will never understand why parents make them go to bed when they're wide awake and make them get up when they're sleepy!

Bernard Brunsting

A CHILD'S VIEW OF LOVE

"When my gran got arthritis, she couldn't bend over and paint her toenails anymore. So my grandpa does it for her all the time, even when his hands got arthritis too. That's love." Rebecca, age eight.

"Love is when you go out to eat and give somebody most of your chips without making them give you any of theirs." Chrissy, age six.

"Love is what makes you smile when you're tired." Terri, age four.

"Love is when my mummy makes coffee for my daddy and she takes a sip before giving it to him, to make sure the taste is okay." Danny, age seven.

"Love is when you tell a guy you like his shirt, and then he wears it every day." Noelle, age seven.

"Love is when Mummy gives Daddy the best piece of chicken." Elaine, age five.

"Love is when your puppy licks your face even after you left him alone all day." Mary Ann, age four.

Author Unknown

Overheard outside the junior section of a public library; two little girls were talking.

One remarked, "Yes, we've moved into a new house now, so my brother and I have a room each."

Then she added thoughtfully: "But Mommy still has to sleep with Daddy."

Nigel Rees

When I was a graduate student, I took my daughter's Montessori school class to a farm near Princeton, New Jersey. Five-year-old Claudia, my daughter's best friend, visiting a farm for the first time, was looking at a fat sow lying in a pen. Said the farmer, "She's mighty big, isn't she?"

"She sure is," said Claudia. "I just saw six little piggies blowing her up a few minutes ago."

Lowell Streiker

A LOGICAL QUESTION

My niece Kim was only three years old. Her sisters, Ronda and Julie, were about five and seven. They lived with their parents, Loren and Penny, and grandparents, my in-laws, better known as Mom and Dad, on a Kansas wheat farm where they also raised cattle.

One Sunday morning, Dad noticed that one of the cows was about ready to birth her calf, and from past experience, he thought she might need some help. So he closed her in a stall in the barn. Then the family went to church.

After church, they all hurried home to see how the cow was doing. Sure enough, she was in hard labor in the barn. So Dad and Loren quickly changed clothes and started out the door to the barn.

"Can we go, Daddy?" asked Ronda.

Looking at Penny, he said, "What do you think?"

"They have to learn sometime," she said. "It might as well be now as later, I guess."

"Okay, let's go then," said Loren, "but you have to stay out of the way so the old cow doesn't kick you."

The birthing process was a long, arduous ordeal, as Dad had suspected it would be. After forty-five minutes of huffing, puffing and using pulling chains, they finally smiled as the little white-faced, spindly-legged calf was born. Dad and Loren, not to mention the cow, were exhausted.

The two men leaned against the barn wall to catch their breath, wipe the sweat off their faces, and admire the wobbly calf. It was at that precise moment that little Kim, peering between the rails of the stall, chose to pose a three-year-old's logical question.

"Well, Daddy," she said seriously. "Just how'd that thing get in there anyway?"

Now if you think Loren was out of breath before, that innocent question really caused him to suck air. But it was, after all, a logical question from a three-year-old viewpoint, don't you think?

Mary Hollingsworth

A group of young children were sitting in a circle with their teacher. She was going round in turn asking them all questions.

"Peter, what noise does a cow make?"

"Moo."

"Anna, what noise does a cat make?"

"Meow."

"Jamie, what sound does a lamb make?"

"Baa."

"Jenny, what sound does a mouse make?"

"Click."

J. John and Mark Stibbe

"You want me to clean my room.
What's my budget for the project?"

THE STAR

There was once a child, and he strolled about a good deal and thought of a number of things. He had a sister, who was a child, too, and his constant companion. These two used to wonder all day long. They wondered at the beauty of the flowers; they wondered at the height and blueness of the sky; they wondered at the depth of the bright water; they wondered at the goodness and the power of God who made the lovely world.

There was one clear shining star that used to come out

in the sky before the rest, near the church spire, above the graves. It was larger and more beautiful, they thought, than all others, and every night they watched for it, standing hand in hand at the window. Whoever saw it first cried out, "I see the star!" And often they cried out together, knowing so well when it would rise and where. So they grew to be such friends with it that, before lying down in their beds, they always looked out once again to bid it good night; and when they were turning around to sleep, they used to say, "God bless the star!"

Charles Dickens

The children bring us laughter,

And the children bring us tears;

They string our joys, like jewels bright,

Upon the thread of years;

In every place where humans toil,

In every dream and plan,

The laughter of the children

Shapes the destiny of man.

Edgar A. Guest

Little Billy was left to fix lunch. When his mother returned with a friend, she noticed that Billy had already strained the tea.

"Did you find the tea strainer?" his mother asked.

"No, Mother, I couldn't, so I used the fly swatter," replied Billy.

His mother nearly fainted, so Billy hastily added, "Don't get excited, Mother. I used an old one."

Bob Phillips

YOU KNOW YOU'RE A KID WHEN . . .

You have to take a bath whether you're dirty or not.

You have to put on a sweater just because your mother is cold.

You have to go to bed early when your dad comes home tired.

You have to eat yucky vegetables because your grandmother says they're good for you.

You can't laugh in church, even when stuff is really funny.

The doctor says, "Now this won't hurt a bit," when you know good 'n' well it's going to hurt like crazy.

A little bit of mud on your dumb suit sends your mom into orbit.

Your dad can stay home from work with a headache, but you have to go to school even when your stomach really hurts.

A cute little lizard in your big sister's backpack gets
you sent to your room for a whole week.

"Time Out" doesn't mean you're at a stopping point in a
football game.

Your feet don't reach the floor from a church pew, but
you get in trouble if you complain about your legs
going numb.

It's always your turn to take out the garbage.

You have to wear somebody else's leftover clothes, but
your mother wouldn't be caught dead in a dress from
the resale shop.

McDonald's is the only place you ever get to go out to
eat.

You can have all the spinach you want, but you can
never have more than one bowl of ice cream.

Mary Hollingsworth

He called a little child and had him stand among them. And
he said: "I tell you the truth, unless you change and become
like little children, you will never enter the kingdom of
heaven. Therefore, whoever humbles himself like this child
is the greatest in the kingdom of heaven.

"And whoever welcomes a little child like this in my
name welcomes me."

Matthew 18:2–5 (NIV)

WHY MOTHERS GET GRAY

A few months ago, I was making several phone calls in the family room, where my three-year-old daughter was playing quietly with her five-month-old brother, Nathan. Nathan loves Adrianne, who has been learning how to mother him gently since he was born.

I suddenly realized that the children were no longer in view. Panic-stricken, I quickly hung up the phone and went looking. Down the hall and around the corner, I found Adrianne and her baby brother playing cheerfully on the floor of the nursery.

Relieved and upset, I shouted, "Adrianne, you know you are not allowed to carry Nathan! He is too little and you'll hurt him if you drop him!"

Startled, she answered, "I didn't, Mommy."

Knowing the baby couldn't crawl, I suspiciously demanded, "Well, then, how did he get all the way into the nursery?"

Confident of my approval for her obedience, she said with a smile, "I rolled him!"

Author Unknown

A little girl said, "My grandmother reads the Bible all day long . . . I think she's cramming for her finals!"

James E. Myers

SPEAKING OF ELECTRICITY

An elementary teacher gave her young class an in-school writing assignment. They were to choose a famous person and write the story of that person's life.

Not wanting to spend an undue amount of time on the assignment, here's what little Jerry wrote about Benjamin Franklin:

Benjamin Franklin was born in Boston. He grew up and moved to Philadelphia. He became a scientist. One day he met a woman on the street. He married her and discovered electricity. The end.

Clyde Shrode

Small children disturb your sleep, big children your life.

Yiddish Proverb

During a children's sermon, Reverend Larry asked the boys and girls what the word "amen" means. Little Chucky's hand shot up, "I know," he chirped. "It means, 'Tha-tha-tha-that's all folks!'"

The World's Greatest Collection of Church Jokes

7

Cash In on Laughter

Money. On its own, it's worthless—just a stack of printed paper, like Monopoly money. What makes it valuable is what we can trade it for, right? But we tend to be really silly about our money—so silly that we do all kinds of crazy things to get it, hang on to it and spend it. And those things are often good for a laugh.

HEY, BROTHER, CAN YOU SPARE A 401(K)?

Many middle-aged people have planned well for retirement. Their savings accounts have grown, their stock investments have paid off and their retirement plans are all set to kick in. They're prepared.

This chapter is for the rest of us. We who have $2.48 in our savings account didn't invest in Microsoft because we thought it was a hand cream and will probably get to our senior years, reach for our nest egg and realize we already fried it years ago.

I've never been much of a financial wizard. The only portfolio I have is the one I bought at OfficeMax. I have, however, watched everyone around me get rich off their stock market or other investments, while I'm busy looking for a grocery store that has a coin machine where I can cash in my quarters.

Not that my husband and I haven't tried our hand at investing. We have. We just haven't been very successful at it. Take, for instance, the piece of desert property we bought over twenty-five years ago as a retirement investment. It's five and a half acres, and we were told it would eventually be worth well over $100,000.

Today, it's not worth much of anything because it has been turned into a sanctuary for an endangered insect. I believe it's in the gnat family. So much for making our fortune there. We've listed it for sale a couple of times, but not many people want to own a government-protected five-and-a-half-acre gnat grazing ground.

Whatever porcelain collectibles I've managed to accumulate over the years haven't paid off either. They actually were increasing in value, but the last Northridge, California, earthquake turned them into mosaic pieces.

How about a game show called *Wheel of Missed Fortunes?* Contestants could spin the wheel for a dollar amount—$10,000, $50,000, $100,000, and so on. A lovely blonde could stand by the answer board

while contestants guessed the cost of their missed investment opportunities or bad business decisions. It might be a
depressing show for the contestants, but the viewing audience would feel a lot better about their own bad investments.

It's hard to predict which "sure deal" really will be a
sure deal. We don't know if a piece of real estate will cost us
a fortune or make us one. The stock market carries no guar-
antees, either. Gold might be devalued; the company han-
dling our retirement account could default; we could be hit
with a catastrophic illness that depletes every dime of our
savings. There are no fail-safe ways to wealth, no assur-
ances that the money we save is going to be there for us
when we need it. That's why the most important investments we can make aren't financial. They are the ones we
make in the lives around us.

Martha Bolton

There was once a congregation that was continually
asked for money; so often, in fact, that they asked
the pastor to speak of them not as his flock but as his
fleeced.

James E. Myers

Some philosophers say that money can't talk, but
I've got news for them—mine speaks quite clearly. It
says, "Good-bye. So long. Farewell. Adieu!"

Mary Hollingsworth

It is difficult to save money when your neighbors keep buying things you can't afford.

Jim Kraus

QUANDARY

If a man runs after money, he's money-mad; if he keeps it, he's a capitalist; if he spends it, he is a playboy; if he doesn't get it, he's a ne'er-do-well; if he doesn't try to get it, he lacks ambition; if he gets it without working for it, he's a parasite; and if he accumulates it after a lifetime of hard work, people call him a fool who never got anything out of life.

Cleon Lyles

A TAXING SITUATION

When I looked at my calendar, a huge red circle around Friday slapped me in the face. Today was Wednesday. I only had two days left to come up with $22,343.70 to pay the IRS, and I had no clue from where that much money could possibly come. My heart was pounding like Thumper the rabbit, sending ominous vibrations to my stressed-out brain. What was I going to do?

I'd already run out of extensions. I'd filed one in April and the second one in August (doesn't everyone?) because I didn't have the money to pay my tax bill. So the jig was up, and I had to face the music. It was do-or-die time, and I could imagine Uncle Sam's finger pointing at me saying, "I want you!"

I had a couple of royalty payments that I'd been trying to collect for months, but those were certainly not forthcoming. Still, I decided to make the call out of sheer desperation.

"Hey, Jerry, this is Mary." And I related to him my dilemma. "Any chance you've received the royalty checks we've been waiting for? I've run out of other options, and I could surely use your help."

"I don't think so, Mary, but I'll check and call you back."

"Okay, Jere. Thanks."

For the next three hours I racked my brain trying to figure out what to do, looking for any kind of resource, praying for help from above. I drummed my fingers, tapped my foot, paced around my office, and generally drove myself crazy thinking of what might happen next. When the phone rang at 4:30, I nearly jumped out of my skin.

"Hello!" I almost yelled.

"Mary, this is Jerry. Well, I think I have a little good news for you. As it turns out, we did receive one of the checks we've been waiting for. It came in yesterday's mail. My accountant just hadn't mentioned it to me."

"Wonderful!" I yelped. "Could you tell me how much my part is and how soon you can get it to me?"

"Yes, your portion is $13,700, and I can overnight it to you today."

"Jerry, have I told you lately that I love you?" I laughed. "You're a lifesaver!"

"I'll get it into FedEx right now, Mary. And I'm glad I could help, at least a little."

"Me too! And thanks so much, Jerry."

"Wahoo! Wahoo!" I chirped as I danced around my office. At least I can send the IRS a token of my esteem and pray they'll be lenient about the rest, I thought. IRS . . . lenient . . . fat chance!

I sat down at my desk and began to fill out the paperwork to submit the partial payment I would be able to make. But my mind was still in turmoil, trying to figure out where I could scrape up another $8,643.70. Do the words "bottom of the barrel" convey what I was feeling?

Needless to say, I slept very little that night, tossing and turning, looking into the inky night, trying to keep my blood pressure under control. And I arose Thursday morning with bleary eyes and cobwebs in my brain from lack of rest. I stumbled to the kitchen, made a pot of strong coffee, knowing I'd probably need it to get through this worrisome day, and poured myself a cup of the black sunshine.

I spent the morning staying as busy as I could to distract myself from the depressing thoughts of being up to my ears in debt to the IRS with little or no prospect of solving the problem.

When FedEx delivered the express letter from Jerry, I took the check directly to the bank to deposit, grabbed a quick hot dog at the Sonic and came back home. I wrote my check for the full $13,700 and started to put it in the IRS envelope when the phone rang.

"Hey, Mary, this is Jerry."

"Hi, Jere. Listen, thanks so much for sending the check. It arrived safely, and I've deposited it. So I can at least pay part of my taxes."

"Well, don't mail that check yet," he said. "Guess what came in my mail today?"

My heart stopped. "No, don't tell me," I said quietly.

"Yes, the other long-awaited royalty check. Can you believe it?" he laughed.

I couldn't even respond. I was so dumbfounded, I was in complete shock.

Jerry went on. "I'll overnight this one to you today so you'll have it in the morning."

"Thanks, Jerry. You can't know what an incredible relief this is. How much is my part of this one?"

I was holding my breath. Would it actually be enough to cover the remaining taxes?

"Your part is $8,650."

It took a few seconds for me to do the mental calculation, and then it registered—God had sent me $6.30 too much! I started to laugh, jump up and down, and dance around the room. I was astounded . . . flabbergasted . . .

> I was . . . flabbergasted . . . that God's timing, as usual, was absolutely perfect.

and so humbled by the realization that God's timing, as usual, was absolutely perfect. "Ask and you will receive" suddenly took on infinitely more meaning to me.

That night, as you can imagine, I slept like a baby. My

blood pressure returned to normal, and my prayers were said with joy.

The second check arrived by FedEx the next morning. So I wrote my check to the IRS and put it in the envelope, which had to be postmarked that day. I went by the bank and made the deposit, then dropped the letter off at the post office with a huge sigh of relief.

Then to celebrate, I drove to Chili's restaurant for lunch. I ordered a cheeseburger, fries and iced tea. As I ate my lunch, I once again thanked God for his grace and generosity. I was still overwhelmed by what had happened.

When I finished my meal, I wiped my hands on my napkin, took out my wallet, and turned over the check. Tears began to roll down my face when I saw that the bill, including the needed tip, came to exactly $6.30.

Mary Hollingsworth

I'm a walking economy. My hairline's in a recession, my waist is a victim of inflation, and together they're putting me in a deep depression.

Joe Taylor Ford

THE LAST NICKEL

A young fellow asked a rich, old businessman how he made his money. The man nodded sagely and said, "It was 1932, the depth of the Great Depression, and I was down to my last nickel.

"I invested that nickel in an apple that I polished all day. At the end of the day, I sold that shiny apple for ten cents.

"The next morning, I invested those ten cents in two apples. I spent the entire day polishing them and sold them for twenty cents. I continued this for a month and accumulated a fortune of $1.37."

"That's amazing," the young man said.

"Then my wife's father died and left us two million dollars."

Jim Kraus

The Lord loveth a cheerful giver.

A guy dies and leaves the shortest will ever. It says, "Being of sound mind, I spent my money!"

Henny Youngman

SQUEEZING IT DRY

A restaurant owner was convinced that his bouncer was the strongest man around. Hand the bouncer a lemon, and he would squeeze it dry. "I'll give one thousand dollars to anyone who can squeeze out one more drop of juice," the owner announced.

There were numerous attempts, but nobody could do it. One day, a scrawny little man came in and asked to try.

The bouncer grabbed a lemon and crushed it with his bare hand before handing the rind to his competitor.

The scrawny man clenched his fist around the lemon and 20 drops fell into the glass!

"How'd you do that?" the owner asked the winner, counting out the money.

"I work for the IRS."

Jim Kraus

ACME LOAN CO.

"They turned me down — another near-debt experience."

A GOOD TEAM

I looked down at the ten dollar bill my husband had handed me as I was finishing up the breakfast dishes. "This will barely cover the new textbook I have to get," I protested.

"What more do you want? I'm working two jobs already," Charlie snapped.

"And all I'm doing is the housework, the cooking and trying to finish my degree. Piece of cake." I grabbed my notebook and stalked out into the rain without another word.

Money, I thought as I drove to the post office to mail my student loan forms. It's always money. Charlie and I used to be so good together, but ever since I'd gone back to school, it felt like all we did was argue about how we were going to make ends meet. When we weren't arguing, it was only because we weren't speaking.

I ran into the post office. By the time I got the forms mailed, class was about to start.

"Miss? Excuse me, miss," someone said as I hurried to my car. An elderly woman waved to me. "Could I trouble you for a ride? I need to take these pills to a friend downtown." She pulled a white pharmacy bag out of a pocket of her old coat.

"I'm sorry," I said, "but—"

> "I prayed for God to send me a kindhearted soul, and when I saw you, I knew you were the one."

"Please, I wouldn't ask unless I really had to," she pleaded. "I prayed for God to send me a kindhearted soul, and when I saw you, I knew you were the one."

Yeah, right, I thought, recalling how nasty I'd just been to my husband. *I'm sure I'm one of God's favorite people today.* In fact, I hadn't felt much of God in my life at all lately. But I couldn't leave this poor lady stranded in the rain. "Okay," I said, "but we have to get a move on."

My companion introduced herself as Mary and, in between giving directions while I drove, she rambled on about herself and her husband. Apparently, they had fallen on hard times. "How about you, dear?" she asked. "Are you married?"

"Yes," I said, not really listening.

"That's wonderful. It's so good to have a partner," she said. "My husband and I don't have much, but we have each other—and of course, our faith in God. Even now, when our heat and hot water are out and we don't have enough for a decent meal, we don't lose heart. We know he watches over us. Look how He sent you to help me today! Oh, right over here, dear." I pulled into her friend's apartment complex.

Suddenly I thought of the ten dollar bill in my purse. *I could borrow the textbook from the library and give her the money instead*, I thought. But all I said was, "Good luck, Mary."

"Thank you, dear," she said, getting out of the car. "God bless you."

All day I kept thinking about Mary. She'd looked worn out. Yet she had found a way to help a sick friend.

She was still on my mind that evening. Sitting at dinner with Charlie, I imagined Mary and her husband in their unheated apartment. We were having a tough time getting by, but at least we were warm. At least we could put food on the table.

While we were doing the dishes, I found myself telling Charlie about Mary. "I know we need that money, but I feel awful," I said. "What if that were us?" All of the frustration and uncertainty of the past months caught up with me. "I'm so turned around about money, I turned my back on someone in need." I started to cry.

Charlie pulled me into his arms. "So what do you want to do?" he asked.

"I'd like to take her some groceries. But I don't even know her last name or where she lives," I said.

"You know where her friend lives, right? It's a start. We'd better hurry before the store closes."

At the grocery store, we zipped down the aisles together, picking up basics. Then Charlie threw in a box of candy; I grabbed some nice soap. When I saw the total on the cash register, I sucked in my breath. Charlie squeezed my hand. "Don't worry," he said. "We'll still be all right."

Charlie drove while I tried to remember the way to Mary's friend's place. *It feels so good to be working together for a change*, I thought as we arrived at the apartment complex.

Inside the lobby was a giant panel with rows of buzzers. Mary had said her friend lived alone, so I started to search for single women's names. My heart sank when I saw that there were no names on the buzzers—just apartment numbers.

"I'm sorry, honey," Charlie said. "At least we gave it a try."

"I know, I know," I sighed, slumping against the wall. *Lord, why isn't anything working out?*

A crackling came from the bank of buzzers. "Hello? Who's there?" a woman's voice asked.

I had accidentally pressed a buzzer when I leaned against the wall. I looked at Charlie.

"Give it a shot," he whispered.

"I'm sorry to bother you," I said. "I'm looking for a lady I gave a ride to today. She was bringing medicine to a friend."

"Oh, you must mean my friend Mary," the woman said. "She was here earlier with my pills."

In no time, we were at Mary's apartment. "Hi, Mary," I said. "I hope we're not disturbing you, but . . ."

". . . We brought you a few things we hope you can use," Charlie continued, carrying in the shopping bags.

"God bless you!" Mary exclaimed. "I'm going to be praying for you two."

We were quiet on the way home. Not the kind of silence that had been coldly punctuating our recent disagreements, but a peaceful, content silence, the kind that can help hold a marriage together.

We were a pretty good team, Charlie and me. We always had been. It just took Mary to remind us.

Donna M. Collins

In every insurance policy the big print giveth and the small print taketh away.

Author Unknown

When it comes to money, always be sure to act your wage.

Dave Ramsey

DAD, I NEED A...WHAT?

The boy was about to turn ten. That's a big age for a kid because they're now close to being a teenager, which is close to being a high schooler, which is close to being a quasi-adult with pimples.

Yeah, turning ten is a pretty big deal.

He tossed a Nerf football in my direction. I snagged the ball close to the tree where the dog does his business and tiptoed into the driveway. At this point, I didn't realize how out of touch I was with the world of today's ten-year-old boy. That would soon change.

I tossed the football back.

"I've been thinking about what I want for my birthday," the Boy said, pulling the ball out of the air.

I smiled. I remembered when I was a kid. Heck, he probably wants a BB gun, a video game, a puppy, a new baseball mitt . . .

"I need a cell phone," he said, tossing the football in a pretty tight spiral.

The ball hit me in the chest and bounced precariously close to the tree.

"What?"

At his age, all I needed for my birthday was a GI Joe with Kung Fu Grip. I didn't need a cell phone.

Okay, okay, so the closest thing to cell phone technology I'd seen as a kid was on Star Trek. The point is I wanted a toy, not a piece of communication equipment capable of connecting me with people who don't even speak English. The only way I'd have possessed something like that as a kid is if I'd been a spy for the Russians . . . which I wasn't.

"I need a cell phone," he said again, running toward me to pick up the ball and toss it back. This time I caught it.

"You don't need a cell phone," I told him. "Cell phones are the gifts that keep on taking. If I buy you a cell phone, we have to keep giving the cell phone company money month after month after month. Besides, cell phones are for adults, Mulder and Scully, teenage girls and crack dealers. You're not a teenage girl, are you?"

"No," he said. "But I still need a cell phone."

I frowned at the boy. The last thing he really, really wanted was Pokémon bed sheets. Now he needs something so he can talk to kids he'll see at school anyway. What will he talk to them about? Probably his really cool Pokémon bed sheets.

I felt the need, as Dad, to use my superior height, weight and upper body strength to put the boy in his place. I threw the Nerf ball like a rocket toward him. He caught it anyway.

"Why do you need a cell phone?" I asked, putting the appropriate stand-up comic emphasis on the word *need*.

"Because kids my age on TV have cell phones."

That's it. I knew cable television would signal the apocalypse.

"Kids your age on TV are secret agents, billionaires and spaceship pilots—all of whom can buy their own cell phones," I said. "When you're one of those, we'll talk."

I threw the ball at him, and he dropped it.

Yeah, the boy's growing up, but Dad's still king.

Jason Offutt

Keep your lives free from the love of money and be content with what you have, because God has said, "Never will I leave you; never will I forsake you."

Hebrews 13:5 (NIV)

Whenever my wife needs money, she calls me handsome. She says, "Hand some over."

Bob Phillips

HOW TO SUCCEED IN BUSINESS...REALLY TRYING

Talk about low man on the totem pole! I couldn't even get near the totem pole during those early years of my driving work. Maybe it hurt so much because I wanted to drive so badly. I had started out driving my daddy's farm truck in Hayneville, Alabama. I was only eleven then, but when I got my hands on that wheel and guided that machine down those red clay ruts, I knew that big truck and I were close friends.

But that old truck wasn't going to take care of eight brothers and sisters. So, soon as I was old enough, I headed for Chicago, where I went to work in a factory. I worked my way up to a good job, but every time I saw a big diesel rig snorting toward the city limits I got the same feeling I'd had as a little boy lying on my cot and hearing the semis double clutch and roar as they bit into the grade on US 31.

Finally, I saved enough money to buy a second-hand tractor rig and started hauling from Chicago to New York, from Cleveland to St. Louis. But I just couldn't make it pay off; the good driving feeling was there, but the money wasn't. Besides, there was something else. I guess it really hit me when I'd see them on the road—those cross-country buses hissing by me in the rain.

In 1958, after moving to New York City, I applied for a job as driver with a charter bus company. They took me on as a standby on the night shift. I got a run only when one of the regular men didn't show up.

Finally I got disgusted and left for another charter

company, but it was just the same. Sometimes I'd buy a run
from a driver, pay him to take his trip and off I'd go under
his name. I'd notice the cost details on
each trip and talk with the dispatcher
and mechanics.

> For I had a dream.
> The only thing was
> it involved twenty-
> five thousand
> dollars.

For I had a dream. The only thing
was it involved twenty-five thousand
dollars. That's what I'd need to buy a
good used bus. And here I was, making thirteen dollars a day as a standby.

But I remembered something my mother always told
me: "It's up to you to take the first step. That shows the
good Lord you're serious about what you want to do, and
then He will help you."

I enrolled in a diesel mechanic's school in Bergenfield,
New Jersey. I paid five dollars a lesson, which lasted from
7:00 PM to midnight, three nights a week. I did this three
years steady until I'd dream about piston rings and crank-
shaft tolerances.

During this time, I started saving in a bank near me.
Every time I saved a hundred dollars, I'd use it to borrow
another hundred and added that to my savings. This way, I
kind of leapfrogged my account ahead. Finally, I had five
thousand dollars. I had a feeling then as if the Lord said,
"Okay, you've taken some steps; now I'm going to show you
a bigger one!"

I heard about a GMC diesel, thirty-seven-passenger bus
for sale at a low figure, low enough to swing it with my

savings and a loan. Only one thing was missing: an engine. Now that mechanic's course would come in handy.

My wife Frankie got a job working in a restaurant, and for the next six months I spent every spare hour with my tool kit, engine manual and an old engine that was little more than junk.

Then came the day I fired it up and, for a minute, I just listened to its music; I got into the driver's seat, and like an uncaged bird, my bus and I hummed along the highway to Brooklyn where I already had a name picked out—B&C Bus Lines.

We'd go to other charter bus companies for jobs. Sure, I still got the leftovers, but now I was driving my own business.

Within two years, I was able to borrow money on this first bus to buy another. By 1965, I had five buses and was providing jobs for people in my neighborhood.

Then the trouble started.

My overhead was climbing like the temperature in some of my radiators. Also, I had no garage and had to park my buses in vacant lots. Just try to fix an engine in the snow!

On top of it all, I was falling behind in my repayments. There was only one earthly thing that could help, and that was money.

One cold morning I walked out to the lot where those five buses sat. One had developed a flat in the night, and I felt as low as that tire. I swung up into the driver's seat of old number one and sat there, wondering if I should just sell out and go back to being last man on the night shift again.

I leaned against that cold steering wheel. *Oh, Lord*, I thought, *I have faith and will take any step. But right now I don't know which direction to take.*

Snow flicked against the windshield. And then I began to get that feeling, the same one I had when I first saw this bus. Only this time it was: "See the Chase Manhattan Bank." I almost laughed out loud. The Chase Manhattan Bank! Maybe if I was Greyhound or US Steel.

But the feeling got stronger. So I contacted the bank.

I couldn't believe it. The man I talked to seemed interested; he wanted to know more about my business. From then on, the bank and I spent a lot of time together. They helped me organize my operations and came through with a loan that not only helped pay off my debts but also enabled me to get a garage.

Today, B&C Bus Lines has fifteen buses on the road. And I like to think we're helping make many people happy—whether we're taking families to a church picnic or a high school class to Washington, DC.

The other day, one of my drivers was ill and I took his run. As my wife, now our office manager, waved me out of the garage, I chuckled; after all this time, it looked like I was still on standby.

As the tires sang beneath me, I thought of the miles that had gone by since I first drove dad's old truck down those clay ruts. And then I thought of mother standing in front of her Sunday school class saying: "Children; you take that first step and the Lord will help you the rest of the way."

"You're so right, Mama," I whispered.

Bill Logan

HIP-HUGGERS

Not every woman can wear this," the salesgirl says as she slips the dress out of my hands and hangs it back on the rack.

If this chick ate a grape, she'd look like a pregnant thermometer. I figure I can take her.

"Look," I say, lifting the dress back off the rack, "this ain't *Pretty Woman* and I'm not Julia Roberts."

"Too bad," the salesgirl says as she jerks the dress out of my hands and hangs it back on the rack. "Because Julia Roberts is a size four, and so is this dress."

I can't tell you what a thrill it is to discover that I was exactly the same size as Julia Roberts—during my first week of fetal formation.

"The main problem is your hips," the salesgirl notes as she scans me up and down using a wide-angle lens. "The rest of you seems fairly normal."

According to *Cosmopolitan*, the scientific journal for women with shoulder pads for brains, I am a "pear." In layman's terms, this means I'm shaped like a wide-body travel mug.

If you go by today's fashions, women with hips are an endangered species. Someday, schoolchildren will gather around my skeleton while a teacher describes that time in history when women with giant hips walked the earth.

"Maybe we could camouflage them somehow," the salesgirl says, tapping her pouty lips with her finger.

Flipping through a rack of comfort-wear, she pulls out a pair of trousers and holds them up to me. The waist is exactly the same diameter as the hips.

"Excuse me," I say. "Do I look like a boa constrictor to you?"

I have an hourglass figure. My waist is fifteen inches smaller than my hips, and my breasts are . . . Okay, so I have a three-minute egg-timer figure.

My point is, if I buy pants that fit my hips, you could park a Volkswagen in the waistband. If I buy pants that fit my waist, I have to buy two pair—one for each thigh.

"Look," I sigh, "surely there is something in this store I can wear."

Coming together in a Halston huddle, all the salesgirls stare at my hips like doctors conferring on how best to separate Siamese twins. "Not a thing," they finally say in unison.

"You're telling me that I'm the only woman left in this world with hips?" I demand.

"You know, they have surgery that can fix that now," the woman at the rack next to me says knowingly.

So this is what it's come to. I'm supposed to have the

meat sucked off my bones in order to attract men who are attracted to women who look like boys.

"Gimme that dress!" I growl through gritted teeth.

Grabbing the hanger off the rack, I make a dash toward the dressing room. Weaving and ducking, I knock emaciated shoppers out of the way like Night of the Living Dead.

Finding an open stall, I run inside, slam the door, and slide the latch. On the wall is a little sign that reads: you stretch it, you buy it.

Kicking off my Reeboks, I drop my jeans to the floor and toss my T-shirt on the hook. Stepping into the dress, I wiggle it into position, suck my belly button to my backbone, and zip. Holding my breath, I take a long, hard look at myself in the mirror.

I'd say it was a perfect fit—if I were an Oscar Mayer wiener. Not only can you see my panty lines, you can identify most of my major organs.

Of course, none of this matters anyway. I just caught a glimpse of the price tag. I can't afford the hanger, much less the dress.

P. S. Wall

People who say money can't buy happiness just don't know where to shop.

Tom Shivers

THAT'S MY MONEY

In 1972, I went to work as a writer on the private staff of "the world's richest man"—oil billionaire H. L. Hunt (the H.L. stands for Haroldson Lafayette.) And it was an experience I'll never forget.

During my tenure with Mr. Hunt, I had a variety of duties and privileges. And I thought you might enjoy hearing a few of them. Naturally, since Mr. Hunt was recognized as having more personal wealth than anyone else on the planet (even by his nearest financial rival, Howard Hughes), money was a huge issue on every front. And his money attracted every kind of virtue and vermin imaginable.

In addition, having that kind of wealth gave Mr. Hunt some unique perspectives on money and how to use it.

The Nickel

It was my privilege one week to fly with Mr. and Mrs. Hunt on their private Lear jet to Hollywood, California, where Mr. Hunt was scheduled to appear on *The Merv Griffin Show*. Merv was hosting a panel of millionaires and Mr. Hunt—a billionaire. Mr. Hunt was, of course, the oldest and richest of the bunch.

We stayed in the Beverly Hills Hotel. In fact, five of us had the entire fifth floor to ourselves. I spent most of my time in the big living room of Mr. and Mrs. Hunt's suite, waiting for him to say, "Jump," so I could respond, "How high?"

One day Mr. Hunt asked me to go down to the lobby to get something for him from the gift shop, which I did. While there, I also made a small purchase for myself. And when I came back to their suite, I had a nickel in my hand—change from my purchase. So I laid it on top of the television until I could return to my own room.

In a little while, Mr. Hunt came through the room and spied the nickel. He looked at it, and then looked back at it. Finally, he said, "Now, who's money is this?"

I laughed and teased him, saying, "Now, Mr. Hunt, that's my nickel, and I need it a lot worse than you do."

He grinned and said, "Well, I'm sure that's right." And he reluctantly walked away, leaving the nickel on the TV.

I'm convinced that, if I had said, "I don't know whose money that is," he would have picked it up and put it in his pocket. In Mr. Hunt's eyes, it seemed that all money was the same because he had so much of it.

Note that he didn't say, "Whose nickel is this?" I believe he would have asked the exact same question if there had been a hundred-dollar bill or a penny. To him, money was money.

Here's another example.

Ice Cream

One day back in Dallas, I was summoned to Mr. Hunt's big corner office. When I arrived, Himself (that's what we called him) had some money in his hand.

"Now, I'd like for you to go get me some ice cream," he

said, and he handed me a one-hundred-dollar bill and a one-dollar bill.

I said, "I'll be happy to, Mr. Hunt," and I took the money and left.

In the outer office, I realized that I couldn't really buy ice cream with either bill. The dollar wasn't enough, and the ice cream store couldn't cash the hundred-dollar bill because it was too large. I had to go downstairs to the bank and get the hundred-dollar bill changed before I could get the ice cream.

Once again, to Mr. Hunt, money was money . . . of any denomination.

> Once again, to Mr. Hunt, money was money . . . of any denomination.

Tipping the Car Hop

One of the jokes in the office was about Mr. Hunt tipping the man in the parking garage for bringing his car around at the end of the day. Even though Mr. Hunt was a billionaire, he always tipped the car hop a quarter. Behind his back, Mr. Hunt's driver gave the guy five dollars, but Mr. Hunt never knew it. And if he had known it, he would probably have been incensed by his driver's extravagance.

Once in a while, Mr. Hunt would realize he didn't have a quarter in his pocket. So he would stop by the office of Welch Wright, his longtime administrator, and borrow a quarter from her. She always gave him the quarter, of course. But he rarely repaid her.

She told me one day that sometimes she would check up

on Himself to see if he was still as alert as he'd always been (he was eighty-three at the time). She would go to his office and say, "Mr. Hunt, may I borrow a quarter for the car hop?" And he would always give it to her. Then she said, without fail, the next morning when he arrived at the office and before he ever went to his office, he stopped at her office and asked for his quarter back. That's how she knew he was still doing well.

Not Worth the Worry

Mr. Hunt's wealth brought the press around on a regular basis, of course. And it was during one of those probing interviews, when reporters tried to make an aging-but-still-brilliant man into a bumbling fool, that Mr. Hunt, as usual, turned the tables on them.

He sat at his desk with a piece of paper in his left hand, his wispy white hair mussed from running his right hand through it, waving the paper to emphasize his answers to their questions.

One reporter baited Mr. Hunt about his sporty son, Lamar, who had bought the Dallas Texans professional football team a couple of years earlier and moved them to Kansas City where they became the Kansas City Chiefs. Predictably, during the transition years, his investment in the team was in the red.

The reporter said, "Mr. Hunt, Lamar has lost over a million dollars a year on a football team. Doesn't that worry you?"

Mr. Hunt paused for a moment, as if mentally calculating, and then said, "Well, the way I figure it, if Lamar lost a million dollars a year, he'd be broke in about four hundred and fifty years." (Lamar was, of course, incredibly wealthy himself.) Then Mr. Hunt grinned his "gotcha" grin, and his blue eyes twinkled with delight as I'd seen them do so often. To the richest man in the world, a million dollars just wasn't worth the worry.

If You've Got It, Flaunt It

Mr. Hunt was a master at getting what he wanted. One incident that proved that was when we traveled to California. We walked into the lobby of the Beverly Hills Hotel and checked in at the registration desk. Mrs. Hunt and the airplane pilots went on to the rooms reserved for us on the fifth floor, but Mr. Hunt turned to me and said, "We'll talk to the bell captain now."

At the time, Mr. Hunt was recovering from recent back surgery. So he had to hold on to my arm to steady Himself, and he could just shuffle his feet along to avoid falling. To any normal observer, in his standard blue suit and bowtie, Mr. Hunt looked like anyone's little old granddaddy and anything but the richest man in the world.

Also, just for background, you need to know that Mr. Hunt was a politically conservative man. And he was not passive about it. In fact, he took a very proactive stance and consistently distributed political comment material both by mail and in person. So when we traveled, we always took boxes of printed literature on political topics with us. It was not unusual for Mr. Hunt, Himself, to put the material on a table in the lobby of the hotel where he was staying and to sit beside the table talking to passersby about his political views. He did not intend for this trip to be an exception.

So we approached the young man behind the stand marked "Bell Captain."

"Young man," said Mr. Hunt politely, "I'd like to put my table up in your lobby."

The young bell captain, unfortunately for him, had no idea who Mr. Hunt was, that he was personal friends with Mr. Hilton, who owned the entire chain of Hilton hotels, or that he had a standing six-foot mahogany table in the lobby of the Dallas Hilton Hotel where his materials were allowed to stay permanently. In fact, someone from our office went to the Hilton and replenished the materials regularly.

So the bell captain responded politely, "Well, I'm sorry, sir, but there's a convention in the hotel, and that really won't be possible."

For about fifteen minutes, Mr. Hunt continued to patiently explain to the young man that it would surely be in his best interest to allow us to put up his table. And for fifteen minutes the young man continued to politely refuse. Meanwhile, I'm standing there, judiciously keeping my mouth shut and thinking, *This should be interesting!*

Finally, Mr. Hunt said, "We'll go to our room now."

I simply said, "Yes, sir." And we turned and walked to the elevator as I was thinking, *This should really be interesting.*

Once in Mr. Hunt's suite, he said to me, "Now, get me Hiltie on the phone."

I dialed the number for Mr. Hilton's Dallas headquarters, asked for Mr. Hilton's secretary, and told her Mr. Hunt wanted to speak to her boss. Instantly, Mr. Hilton came on the line.

"Mr. Hilton," I said, "I have Mr. Hunt for you."

"Well, put him on!"

I handed Mr. Hunt the phone, saying, "It's Mr. Hilton."

With no greeting or small talk, Mr. Hunt said, "Hilt, I'm in your hotel out here in California, and they won't let me put my table up in the lobby."

I turned toward the window to keep from laughing, thinking, *Yep, this is going to be very interesting.* Of course, I could only hear Mr. Hunt's side of the conversation, so I don't know what Mr. Hilton said. The next thing I heard was this:

"Now, Hilt, you know I've been known to buy hotels." Click! Mr. Hunt hung up.

I almost choked to keep from laughing out loud.

In less than five minutes, there was a knock on the door.

I opened the door, and there stood a very red-faced bell captain.

"Mr. Hunt, we have your table up in the lobby!"

I learned some great lessons about money from the world's richest man. And they have served me well through the years.

Mary Hollingsworth

A generous man will prosper; he who refreshes others will himself be refreshed.

Proverbs 11:25 (NIV)

TAX PREPARATION SERVICE

"Why, I couldn't have done a better job myself — that'll be $750.00."

Money—if you'll excuse the expression—is like manure. It's not worth anything unless it is spread around to make things grow!

Hello, Dolly!

THANKS ANYWAY!

A little boy needed one hundred dollars for a school field trip, so his mother told him to ask God for it. He prayed for two weeks, but nothing turned up. So he decided to ask God for the money in a letter.

At the post office, the postmaster opened the letter to God and decided to forward it to the President of the United States.

The President was charmed, so he told his secretary to send the boy five dollars. After receiving the money, the boy wrote a thank-you letter to God.

"Dear God, Thank you very much for sending the money. I noticed that you had to send it through Washington. As usual, those guys deducted ninety-five dollars. Thanks anyway!"

Jim Kraus

The buck stops here!

A sign on the desk of
President Harry S. Truman

8

Holiday Hilarity

Santa Claus. Easter bunnies. Red, white and blue decorations. Fun and frivolity! We just love our holidays. Some of our best memories and favorite times center around them. They're also perfect times for disasters and sheer delirium, and hysteria breaks out.

TOOTHLESS GRIN

I was doing some shopping in a toy store and decided to look at fashion dolls. A nicely dressed little girl was excitedly looking through the same dolls as well, with a roll of money clamped tightly in her little hand. When she came upon a doll she liked, she would turn and ask her father if she had enough money to buy it. He usually said "yes," but she would keep looking and keep going, through their ritual of "Do I have enough?"

As she was looking, a little boy wandered in across the aisle and started sorting through some of the video games. He was dressed neatly, but in clothes that were obviously rather worn, and wearing a jacket that was probably a couple of sizes too small. He, too, had money in his hand, but it looked to be no more than five dollars or so, at the most. He was with his father as well, but each time he picked one of the video games and looked at his father, his father shook his head.

The little girl had apparently chosen her doll, a beautifully dressed, glamorous creation that would have been the envy of every little girl on the block. However, she had stopped and was watching the interchange between the little boy and his father. Rather dejectedly, the boy had given up on the video games and had chosen what looked like a book of stickers instead. He and his father then started walking through another aisle of the store.

The little girl put her carefully chosen doll back on the shelf and ran over to the video games. She excitedly picked up one that was lying on top of the other toys and raced toward the checkout after speaking with her father. I picked up my purchases and got in line behind them. Then, much to the little girl's obvious delight, the little boy and his father got in line behind me.

After the toy was paid for and bagged, the little girl handed it back to the cashier and whispered something in her ear. The cashier smiled and put the package under the counter. I paid for my purchases and was rearranging things in my purse when the little boy came up to the cashier.

The cashier rang up his purchases and then said, "Congratulations, you have been selected to win a prize!" With that, she handed the little boy the video game, and he could only stare in disbelief. It was, he said, exactly what he had wanted!

The little girl and her father had been standing at the doorway during all of this, and I saw the biggest, prettiest, toothless grin on that little girl that I have ever seen in my life. Then they walked out the door, and I followed, close behind them.

As I walked back to my car, in amazement over what I had just witnessed, I heard the father ask his daughter why she had done that. I'll never forget what she said to him. "Daddy, didn't Nana and PawPaw want me to buy something that would make me happy?" He said, "Of course they did, honey." To which the little girl replied, "Well, I just did!" With that, she giggled and started skipping toward their car.

Sharon Mason Palmer

PUNXSUTAWNEY?

Holiday break was over, and the teacher was asking the class about their vacations. She turned to one boy and asked him what he did over the break.

"We went to visit my grandmother in Punxsutawney, Pennsylvania," he replied.

"That sounds like an excellent spelling word," the teacher said. "Can you tell the class how you spell that?"

Without hesitating, he said, "You know, come to think of it, we went to New York City."

Jim Kraus

THE JOYS OF EASTER

Marshmallow eggs

And jelly beans,

A friendly Easter bunny,

Ribboned baskets,

Flower bonnets,

A day so bright and sunny,

Pink plush rabbits,

Yellow ducks,

Easter lilies fair,

Hyacinths, tulips

Blooming everywhere—

The earth is rain washed,

Born again;

The lark and robin sing,

And, blessed Lord,

We thank You for

The joys that Easter brings.

Violet Bigelow Rourke

THE ONE THING WE ALL WANT

What is Easter? Is it a day when everybody dresses up? Is it a holiday? Is it flowers? Is it the end of winter and the coming of spring? Oh yes, it is all of these. But these are only signs of the main thing. What Easter really demonstrates is the one thing we all want—life. Easter promises us life, now and always.

Easter promises us life, now and always.

One dark, gloomy, rainy morning while I was on a speaking trip, I went into a hotel coffee shop in an Indiana town. I took a seat at a table for two and noticed a man at the door with a look of happiness on his face. The hostess brought the man over to my table and asked if I minded if he sat with me and, of course, I welcomed him. We were by the window and you could hear the drumming of the rain outside. But he greeted me by saying, "Isn't this a terrific morning!"

"Well, yes, I guess it is," I said. "It's raining, though."

"Ah, yes," he continued, "but look at the raindrops glistening like diamonds. Isn't it beautiful?" Then he changed the subject. "You know, there is something marvelous about breakfast in a hotel dining room, isn't there?"

Well, I am an enthusiastic person, but I figured this was really putting it on a bit thick. So I said, "I'm interested in your vibrant attitude. You seem so alive. How did you get this way?"

"Well, sir," he answered, "some time ago I was in a serious accident. While the doctors were working on me in the hospital, I could hear a voice saying, 'There isn't much chance for this fellow.' And even in my bewildered state I thought, *Oh, I don't want to die!*

"It was touch and go for days, but, by the grace of God, I got well. And now it is all so different, so unbelievably wonderful. It's as if I never really lived before. People are beautiful; the world is beautiful; even simple things are exciting."

What had happened to this man was that he had experienced a new awareness of life, a deeper sensitivity. A keen delight had been put upon this thing called life.

Easter comes to remind us that life is not just for now, it is forever. Jesus said, "Because I live, ye shall live also" (John 14:19, KJV). He was telling us that life has two sides, this side and the other side.

But the Resurrection is much more than a single event that happened over two thousand years ago. It is also a contemporary process whereby the spiritually dead, the unhappy, the sinful, the weak, find new life through Jesus.

Life can be ordinary, or it can be great. Easter is a perfect time to wake up and become enthusiastically alive, knowing that because He lives, we may live also.

Norman Vincent Peale

DO YOU KNOW BAILEY'S JESUS?

God recently allowed me to see Jesus through the eyes of someone seeing Him for the first time. Having the advantage of knowing how The Story ends, we can easily forget the cost of our redemption and the love of our Savior. We can get so caught up in holidays and shopping and parties, with Santa and the trappings that we miss the Message, we miss the Messiah.

Every year we attend a local church pageant at

Christmas time, which tells the story of Jesus from His birth through His Resurrection. It is a spectacular event, with live animals and awesome special effects and sets. Dozens of cast members portray angels, shepherds, priests and peasants using the entire auditorium to reenact the story. The audience turns, lifting children in the air, straining to see, as from the rear of the huge auditorium, the exotic magi appear in brilliant colors on llamas or carried by servants, descending the steps in pomp and majesty. Roman soldiers look huge and menacing in their costumes and makeup. The angelic host is breathtaking, hanging suspended in the heavens.

Of all the years we have attended, one stands out indelibly in my heart. It was the year we took our then three-year-old granddaughter, Bailey, who loves Jesus. She was mesmerized throughout the entire play, not just watching, but involved as if she were a player. She watched as Joseph and Mary traveled to Bethlehem and was thrilled when she saw the baby Jesus in His mother's arms.

When Jesus, on a young donkey, descended the steps from the back of the auditorium, depicting His triumphal entry into Jerusalem, Bailey was ecstatic. As he neared our aisle, Bailey began jumping up and down screaming, "Jesus, Jesus! There's Jesus!" Not just saying the words but exclaiming them with every fiber of her being. She alternated between screaming His name and hugging us. "It's Jesus. Look!" I thought she might actually pass out. Tears filled my eyes as I looked at Jesus through the eyes of a child in love with Him, seeing Him for the first time. How like the blind beggar screaming out in reckless abandon, "Jesus, Jesus!" afraid he might miss Him, not caring what others thought (see Mark 10:46-52). This was so much fun watching her watching him.

But then came the arrest scene. On stage, the soldiers shoved and slapped Jesus as they moved Him from the Garden of Gethsemane to Pilate. The sounds of whips and slaps reverberated.

Bailey stood and responded as if she were in the crowd of women, with terror and anger. "Stop it!" she screamed. "Bad soldiers, stop it!"

As I watched her reaction, I panicked. I wished we had talked to her before the play. I realized she didn't know how The Story ends. "Bailey, it's okay. They are just pretending."

"They are hurting Jesus! Stop it!" She stood in her seat reacting to each and every move.

People around us at first smiled at her reaction, thinking, *How cute.* But it wasn't cute; it was a child who knew only that her Jesus, who loves the little children, was being hurt. Her world was crumbling. Isn't that what those first disciples must have felt, and Mary too? I began to notice the people around us quit smiling and began watching her watch Him, almost as if they were afraid not to.

In a most powerful scene, the soldiers led Jesus carrying the cross down the steps of the auditorium from the back. They were yelling, whipping and cursing at Jesus, who was bloodied and beaten.

Bailey was now hysterical. "Stop it! Soldiers! Stop it!" she screamed. She must have been wondering why all these people did nothing. She then began to cry instead of scream, "Jesus, oh, Jesus!"

> She then began
> to cry instead
> of scream,
> "Jesus, oh, Jesus!"

People all around us began to weep as we all watched this devoted little disciple see her Jesus beaten and killed as those first-century disciples had. "Why doesn't someone do something?" I will never forget the face of the gentleman in front of us as he sat watching her with tears streaming down his face.

Going back and forth between her mother's lap and mine, she was not to be comforted.

We kept saying, "Bailey, it's okay. Jesus is going to be okay. These are just people pretending to be soldiers." She looked at me like I was crazy. "Jesus . . ." she cried. In my lap, we talked through the cross and burial. "Watch, Bailey, watch for Jesus!"

At last the tomb began to tremble and lightening flashed as the stone rolled away. A million-person-superbowl-touchdown-cheer couldn't come close to matching this little one's reaction to the Resurrection. "Jesus! He's okay, Mommy, it's Jesus! Look! He's okay!" People all around us cheered!

I prayed that Bailey wasn't going to be traumatized by this event, but that she would remember it. I shall never forget it. I shall never forget seeing Jesus' suffering,

Crucifixion and Resurrection through the eyes of an innocent child.

Following the pageant the actors all assembled in the
foyer to be greeted by the audience. As we passed by some
of the soldiers, Bailey screamed out, "Bad soldier, don't you
hurt Jesus."

The actor who portrayed Jesus was some distance away
surrounded by well-wishers and friends. Bailey broke away
from us and ran toward him, wrapping herself around his
legs, holding on for dear life.

He hugged her and said, "Jesus loves you." He patted
her to go away. She wouldn't let go. She kept clinging to
Him, laughing and calling His name. She wasn't about to let
go of her Jesus.

I think God in heaven stopped whatever was going on
that day and made all the angels watch Bailey. "Now, look
there! You see what I meant when I said, 'Of such is the
kingdom of heaven'?"

Bailey's reaction should be our reaction every day.
When we think of Him—who He is, what He did for us, and
what He offers us—how can we do anything less than wor-
ship Him?

Ginger Tucker

**September 8 is a holiday in Beverly Hills. That's the
day the new Mercedes comes out.**

Milton Berle

"I stopped making a list. Nothing is considered naughty anymore!"

YOU KNOW IT'S MOTHER'S DAY WHEN . . .

Mother's Day is that special day when we show our mothers how much they're loved. You'll know it's here when:

- A delivery man appears at your door with a dozen red roses, and he's not lost.

- Your children tell you how wonderful you are, and they're not setting you up for an allowance increase.

- You get served breakfast in bed. (Up till now the only way for you to get breakfast in bed was to sleep with a Twinkie under your pillow.)

- You notice your kids are hiding a card behind their backs, and it's not report card day.

- Your eldest son, the college student, appears at your door; but today, the little bundle in his hand is for you, not your washing machine.

- Not one of your kids asks you to drive them anywhere for anything. (But since this is the first time in a year you've been able to turn off your car's engine, you find the key has rusted in place!)

- You get thanked for all the little things moms do throughout the year—you know, like cooking, cleaning, helping with homework, saving the universe . . .

- For the first time in months, you get taken to a restaurant where the "catch of the day" refers to their fish specialty, not how well you caught your order as your drove by their drive-up window.

- Your husband promises not to watch any sports events on television all day . . . as long as the game comes in clearly on his two stereos, ham radio and Walkman.

- But most of all, you know it's Mother's Day when your family tells you what a loving, kind, warm-hearted person you are, and no one brought home a new pet!

Martha Bolton

THE INSCRIPTION

Little Johnny had bought Grandma a book for her birthday and wanted to write a suitable inscription. He racked his brain until, suddenly, he remembered that his father had a book with an inscription of which he was very proud, so Johnny decided to copy it. You can imagine Grandma's surprise when she opened her book, a Bible, and found neatly inscribed the following phrase: "To Grandma, with compliments of the author."

John and Mark Stibbe

MAYONNAISE CRAZE

Most people don't know that back in 1912, Hellmann's mayonnaise was manufactured in England. In fact, the Titanic was carrying twelve thousand jars of the condiment scheduled for delivery in Veracruz, Mexico, which was to be the next port of call for the great ship after its stop in New York.

This would have been the largest single shipment of mayonnaise ever delivered to Mexico. But as we know, the great ship did not make it to New York. The ship hit an iceberg and sank, and the cargo was forever lost.

The people of Mexico, who were crazy about mayonnaise and were eagerly awaiting its delivery, were disconsolate at the loss. Their anguish was so great that they declared a national day of mourning, which they still observe to this day.

The national day of mourning occurs each year on May 5 and is known, of course, as Sinko de Mayo.

Author Unknown

TRICK OR TREAT!

The door bell rings, and a man answers it. Here stands this plain but well-dressed kid saying, "Trick or treat!"

The man asks the kid what he's dressed up like for Halloween.

The kid says, "I'm an IRS agent." Then he takes twenty-eight percent of the man's candy, leaves and doesn't say thank you.

Author Unknown

THE PERK FROM ABOVE

Several years ago I was driving down a rain-swept street in Long Beach, California, on an errand from my office. It was cold, the day was dreary, the sky was overcast, I couldn't find the address I was seeking and my spirit was out of sorts. I hadn't wanted to leave the comfort of a warm office, but I had no choice. You know how it goes—the demands of duty. As I was driving along, fretting about a problem that was sapping my emotional energy, I said to God, "Lord, would You please give me a perk? Some little something to lift my spirit?

Doesn't have to be big. Doesn't have to be flashy. Just do something creative to cheer me up and to remind me that I'm glad I'm alive. I'd appreciate that very much."

At that moment I turned the corner, looked to my left, and there in the cab of a pickup truck sat two clowns. They were fully decked out in clown regalia, complete with red woolen yarn hair, big bow ties, painted faces, and each holding a helium-filled balloon. As I looked at them, they simultaneously turned, looked at me and flashed toothless grins from ear to ear. What a unique answer to prayer. I absolutely loved it, and all alone in my car I yelled, "All right! Great perk, Lord. What an idea. How clever You are. Who would ever have thought of two clowns in a pickup?"

Luci Swindoll

In kindergarten, they were getting tuned up for the Fourth of July. Each child had a part in the informal presentation. One little girl said, "This is the flag of my country."

"What is your country?" asked a visiting adult.

"'Tis of thee," she replied.

Helen and Larry Eisenberg

THE TOWN THAT REMEMBERS

The parade stepped off at exactly 11:00 AM from in front of the old firehouse, though the Cub Scouts and Brownies couldn't seem to get themselves in a straight line.

It surely didn't matter. As the motorcycles and color guard led the group down the highway onto Main Street, past wide-eyed youngsters perched like birds at the street's edge, people decades too old and years too young to be Scouts joined the young marchers, walking alongside, riding bicycles, some even on horseback. By the time they all passed the general store and reached the little post office, it was the biggest Memorial Day parade the little Massachusetts town had ever seen. "Why couldn't it always have been this way?" one Cub asked his friend.

Why indeed? For you see, despite Savoy's long history of remembering its war dead, despite a venerable white wooden roster that bore the name of each of the town's service veterans, from the Revolutionary War to Vietnam, Memorial Day had fallen into disuse, just as it had in many, many towns and cities all across America. For many people in Savoy, the three-day weekend seemed better suited for a trip to the mountains of nearby New York or Vermont.

> Would he too have been forgotten, as the other veterans from Savoy had been?

And that bothered Althea Maynard, for twenty years the postmistress of the town. Her son had been in Vietnam, and although he had come home safely, Althea often wondered what might have happened if he hadn't. Would he too have been forgotten, as the other veterans from Savoy had been?

Althea often tried to reinstitute some kind of Memorial Day celebration, with no success, until one day she happened to mention her frustrations to a group of her friends at Savoy Baptist Church.

"Well, why can't we plan a celebration ourselves?" was their reply.

So a committee was established, plans drawn up. Althea made some phone calls and arranged for a speaker. The grass around the memorial roster was delicately trimmed.

And, suddenly, all those people who had been too busy for Memorial Day were caught up in its spirit. They joined Althea and her friends at parade's end, in front of the roster, as the flag was raised; they listened attentively as two elementary students read the Gettysburg Address and "In Flanders Field"; together they bowed their heads when, first hesitantly, then with a firmness that belied the beads of perspiration on his forehead, a Scout played "Taps." They stood at attention as the American Legionnaires fired a volley over the newly flag-and-flower-decorated grave.

It was all over quite quickly, for even the biggest parade and program in a town of 478 persons isn't all that big. But for Althea Maynard, and for the rest of Savoy, the spirit of Memorial Day would last the rest of the year. The spirit of remembering the freedom their sons had fought so hard to preserve, freedom that lives on far past a parade. And the hope that "One Nation Under God" would never for them become an empty promise.

Savoy, Massachusetts, is a town that remembers once again. Will you be thanking God for your heritage of freedom this Memorial Day?

Guideposts

SOMETHING A LITTLE DIFFERENT

It was one of those holidays—you know, the holiday that your mother and grandmother get together and declare that, this year, they are going to enjoy Thanksgiving and not cook. Of course, we all thought they were joking, and to placate them, we just nodded our heads. Why not? It was October and almost two full months away from the most important day—the beginning of the feasting season.

November dawned bright and crisp. Our house was bustling with thoughts of future overloaded plates of turkey, dressing and cranberry sauce. Well, almost everyone's thoughts were headed in that direction. Unbeknownst to my father and siblings, my mother and grandmother had already made plans for Thanksgiving Day. One week before the big day, Mom sat us all down to deliver the news.

"We are all going to go eat Thanksgiving dinner at Pep, a quaint German town. The entire town turns out for Thanksgiving and eats together," Mom explained very calmly.

"Why?" My brother was the first to ask the most sensible question each of us was thinking.

"Well," Mom went on, "Nana (that's my grandmother)

and I thought it would be a nice change for us to not cook and for the family to experience some-thing new and different."

"Couldn't we have a different kind of pie or cake as a new experience instead?" I asked, hoping against hope that I was just dreaming. Thoughts of leftovers were fleeting fast.

> "Couldn't we have a different kind of pie or cake as a new experience instead?"

"No, we are all going to drive to Pep together and eat Thanksgiving dinner there with the rest of the town. However, we'll go back to Nana's house to have pumpkin pie."

My three siblings and I tried to talk Mom out of this plan; my dad had already wisely given in. We tried explaining to her how important it was for us in our tender years to have traditions—turkey and leftovers being some of them. However, it was no use. She was determined to try something new this year, and this was it.

Thanksgiving Day arrived bathed in bright sunshine and cool temperatures. We all dressed accordingly and piled into the family van. Our first stop was to pick up Nana, who lived an hour's drive away. Then we headed toward Pep. On the way, Mom regaled us with information about the town —how the tradition of serving Thanksgiving dinner to the community and beyond started in 1945, and how the town of Pep grew, for that one day, three hundred times its size from all those who went to eat at the community center there.

Stepping out of the van, we all stopped short. In front of the main community center, where the dinner was being held, we saw a line of people that wrapped around the entire building. After asking a few questions from some passersby, we got in line to wait for our entrance into the dining area.

The day was cool, and none of us had expected to wait outside, so needless to say, our wait wasn't the most pleasant. To keep our thoughts uplifted, Mom interjected, "Look on the bright side, at least it isn't raining or snowing while we wait outside."

Of course, we all gave her "the look" as if to say, "We didn't want to be waiting at all, but to be in Nana's house watching football and seeing her and Nana cook." But that was last year, and this was this year.

Once inside the building, we were instructed to get a tray, similar to what is used in public school cafeterias, and go to where plates of food were being prepared. We found a table with enough places for the seven of us. After saying the blessing, we started eating. The food wasn't too bad—not Mom's cooking—but palatable. Being a German town, there was also sausage and sauerkraut—not your normal Thanksgiving fare, but interesting nonetheless.

Since there was no table to clear or dishes to wash, our dining experience was short-lived. That, and we needed to move on since there were others outside waiting in the cold for a place to sit and eat.

We all thanked the citizens of Pep for a memorable time

and got in the van. Heading back to Nana's for the one thing that was still familiar—Mom's pumpkin pie—conversation turned toward what had just taken place.

Being the eldest child, I took it upon myself to be the spokesperson for the group. "Mom, thank you for having us try something new and different this year. It was definitely new and different. However, if you want to do it again, you'll have to go alone. But we still love you for the experience."

Being the wise woman she is, she understood where we were coming from and vowed to never try something new or different during the holidays again. After all, traditions are important, they make families—well, families. They are the ties that bind.

Rhonda Hogan

WHERE THERE'S SMOKE, THERE'S TURKEY

A few years ago Mark Lowry sent me a smoked turkey for Christmas. It was, according to his enthusiastic endorsement, some of the best turkey in the world. Unfortunately, I didn't get to test that claim because I didn't take time to read the directions. Not knowing the word "smoked" meant "fully cooked," I assumed I should roast the bird the same way I do all my turkeys: in a 350-degree oven until tender, or until the firemen arrive, whichever comes first.

For the entire time that turkey was roasting, everything seemed to be going fine. There weren't any dark clouds billowing out of the oven. There was no odor of burning meat. My smoke alarm didn't even go off.

But when I finally took that poor bird out of the oven, some fourteen hours later, and pulled back the aluminum foil covering it, I couldn't believe my eyes. The poor thing looked as if it'd been struck by lightning! Twice! It was as black as a pair of army boots and about as tender. Its poor legs were pointing in opposite directions, and the meat on each drumstick had shrunk, leaving four inches of bare bone protruding in the air. Had the ASPCA seen it, I'd still be paying off the fine!

Martha Bolton

A lady was picking through the frozen turkeys at the grocery store but couldn't find one big enough for her family.

She asked a stock boy, "Do these turkeys get any bigger?"

The stock boy replied, "No ma'am, they're dead."

Author Unknown

WHATEVER HAPPENED TO CHRISTMAS?

When I was a kid, at Christmas you piled all the presents in the car, loaded up Rags the dog, and drove about thirty minutes to Grandmother and Granddaddy's house in the country. There were thirty people there—kids, grandkids, cousins, aunts and uncles, three dogs, a mouthy Siamese cat, two turtles and a white hamster named Harry. And we all spent the night . . . in beds, on pallets, on sofas, in the dining room, in the living room, or on any square inch of floor that wasn't already occupied. It was such fun!

My grandmother's Christmas tree was a wonderful treat all on its own. She decorated it with snowmen and Santas made of yarn, candy canes, gum sticks, popcorn and cookies hung on loops of sewing thread. Each grandchild could have one . . . and only one . . . treat per day until Christmas Day (unless you could sneak in undetected and swipe an extra one when the adults weren't looking); then we got to finish it all off in one delicious frenzy on Christmas Day.

My grandparents' house was unique. It had an outdoor porch that ran right through the middle of the house under the roof from north to south and all across the south end of the house, making a T-shaped porch. There were five rooms to the house—the kitchen, the dining room, "the house" (my grandparents' combo bedroom and living room), the "East room" (a large bedroom with three full-size beds and a postage-stamp-size closet), and the "little room" (about five feet wide and twelve feet long with one small, metal army cot and a big, wooden quilt closet stacked from floor to ceiling with handmade quilts my grandmother had made).

Each of the five rooms had an outside wooden door and screen door that opened onto the north-south porch—three rooms on one side and two on the other. In the winter, all the doors remained closed, but in the summer, the wooden doors were left open so the breeze could circulate through the house.

That porch was the gathering place for family and friends in the summertime. Everyone would drag rocking chairs onto the porch where we sat, rocked, shelled peas or peeled peaches, talked, laughed and enjoyed the cool north breeze that inevitably wafted through the eight-foot-wide corridor. The porch was invariably strewn with vegetable baskets, baby pallets, left-behind sneakers and pets—it was the place to be and the setting of many fond memories for me.

"The stockings were hung from the chimney with care" ... everywhere! There were dozens of stockings, hand-made and decorated with each individual in mind. And the anticipation of seeing them bulging on Christmas morning with special ribbon candy, nuts, fruit and tiny toys was almost too much to bear.

My cousins Denise and Donna and I all slept together in one of the beds in the East room. We would lie there listening with all our might, knowing that any minute we would hear the bells on Santa Claus's sleigh and his reindeer on the rooftop. If we whispered about it, we got shushed by our parents in the other beds in the room. So we agonized in silent anticipation until we fell asleep.

The next morning, awakened by Granddaddy's old banty rooster, Chuckles, we would leap out of bed onto the frigid linoleum floor, grab our robes and house shoes, and race across the freezing-cold porch to "the house" where the cedar Christmas tree stood atop Grandmother's old library table in the corner. Grandmother and Granddaddy had been up for ages, of course, and we could smell biscuits and gravy, coffee, and bacon cooking in the kitchen.

Then our eyes would pop when we saw presents galore under the tree and on the floor all around. Presents for thirty people looked like an explosion at Macy's! And we began nosing around to see which presents had our names on them. We weren't allowed to shake them, though. No, sir! All we could do was look.

Then one of the cousins would shout, "Hey, look! The stockings!"

And we would all rush to the fireplace to peek in the tops of our stockings to see if we could tell what was in them. We couldn't open them right away because, at Grandmother's, everything had a proper order, and breakfast came before anything else. But before we had breakfast, we had to go to the outhouse and then wash our hands.

Now, going to the outhouse on Christmas morning in thirty-degree weather was not a delight that we relished, no matter how badly we needed to go. The trick was to run as fast as you could, back up to the north wind and do your business as fast as you could, and run back to the house as fast as you could. Then you hurried (no running allowed in the house) to the living room and backed up to the fireplace to warm up that which had been exposed to the elements. Once you were sufficiently warmed up, then you went to wash your hands.

And that brings up another real country delight in the winter—drawing rain water from the brick cistern out on the north end of the porch with the wind whistling up your pajama legs. Yahoo! I can still hear the squeak of the old rope pulley as you let the galvanized bucket down into the cistern and pulled up the pail of freezing water. If you were little, either an adult or an older cousin had to help you do it because a bucket of water is very heavy.

Taking the bucket into the kitchen, some of the cold water was poured into the white-metal wash pan. Grandmother would add a little boiling water from the teakettle to the wash pan to warm the water. Then, finally, you could wash your hands. It seemed that everything in the country was a process. You couldn't just turn on the tap and get hot water as we do today.

Then everyone sat down to breakfast. The adults all ate first; then we kids got what was left, although there was always plenty to go around. I remember we laughed a lot, told funny stories about Christmases past, relived family reunions and tried to guess what was in our presents. Needless to say, our imaginations and wish lists were far greater than Santa's budget.

> Needless to say, our imaginations and wish lists were far greater than Santa's budget.

"Is it time to open the presents now?" a little one would ask.

"Not yet, sweetheart," said Grandmother. "First, we need to do the dishes and clean up the kitchen."

"Aw, shucks."

"Well, if everyone helps, it will only take a few minutes."

Man, we were out of our seats and carrying dishes to the kitchen in a flash. We scraped the leftovers into the slop bucket for the hogs and stacked the small plates on top of the big plates. While the women did the dishes, the men took all the chairs from the dining room and kitchen into "the house" where we would open our presents. Meanwhile, we kids found a strategic place near the Christmas tree where we could sit on a rug on the floor or stand beside the bed to open our gifts. And we waited . . . not too patiently . . . for the ladies to arrive.

After what seemed an interminable period of time, our moms and aunts would come in and find a chair. Finally . . . finally, Grandmother would come in, wiping her hands on her apron and say, "Well, we'd best get at it. You kids come and get your stockings." And she would hand them to us one by one. The parents would laugh and watch as we dug to the bottom of our stockings, delighting in every tiny treasure we found.

When the stockings had been thoroughly investigated, Grandmother would say, "Frank, will you please play Santa and hand out the presents?" (Frank is the eldest grandchild and my brother.)

Now, Christmas in our family is not just a rip-and-tear event. Instead, because there were so many of us and because we drew names, Grandmother thought we should take the time for everyone to see what each person received.

It also gave us a chance to thank properly the person who had drawn our name.

So Frank would dig through the presents until he found one for each person in the room. Then, starting with the youngest child (because he had the least amount of patience), we opened the gifts one by one and showed everyone what we had received, thanking the appropriate person. Then Frank would start again, and we would repeat the process until all the presents were gone. It took forever! But we loved it because it made Christmas last a lot longer. In fact, we still do it that way in our family today.

Another habit our family had was saving the wrapping paper. Bows and ribbons went in one bag, and paper was carefully removed (not ripped), folded gently and put in a stack. Grandmother put the paper into a special box with a lid and saved it until the next December. Then she took it out of the box and ironed the paper and the ribbon to remove the wrinkles and folds and wrapped packages in it again. Some of that wrapping paper was around for years! We would laugh and say, "Hey, that was my present last year!"

Presents were different in those days, too. Instead of one-size-fits-all electronic Sudoku games and battery-operated, life-size robots that cost a fortune, we received simple gifts. Handmade. Personalized. Carefully chosen just for you. Things like crocheted doilies, quilts, dresses or shirts made out of flour-sack material, homemade dolls and stuffed animals, homemade soap and candles, canned peaches and green beans, underwear (always underwear!), and potholders. I still have a little patchwork jacket that my grandmother made for me out of material scraps. It's very special to me because she died when I was in the third grade, and it's one of the few things I have from her.

When, at last, the presents were all unwrapped, lunch was finished and the dishes were done, we began packing up to leave. We gave our cousins hugs, kissed our grandparents good-bye, thanked everybody again for the wonderful gifts, loaded up the car and started home. And before we got to the end of the lane, we kids fell asleep from the sheer exhausted delight of it all, dreaming of next Christmas when we'd all be together again.

Whatever happened to Christmases like that anyway?

Mary Hollingsworth

AIRPORT GRANDMA

When I stopped the bus to pick up Chris for nursery, I noticed an older woman hugging him as he left the house.

"Is that your grandmother?" I asked.

"Yes," Chris said. "She's come to visit us for Christmas."

"How nice," I said. "Where does she live?"

"At the airport," Chris replied. "Whenever we want her, we just go out there and get her."

John and Mark Stibbe

WHAT GOES UP MUST COME DOWN

There's an old saying that has always inspired.
Three little words . . . "No assembly required!"

I will never forget the Christmas we bought our sons a new swing set. My husband stayed up all night Christmas Eve putting it together. It would have gone faster, but he insisted on doing it the hard way—by reading the "easy to assemble" directions. The directions were about twenty-five pages long and written in four different languages (none of them English).

The only set of instructions that bore a faint resemblance to our native tongue read as follows: "Insert A into C, bypass B until Step #4, then connect G-1 to D-4, bringing Fig. 8 into alignment with J-7 and overlapping M-3 and P-6. Adjust R-5 to compensate for the 6H4 adjustment."

Since it was too late in the evening to hire an interpreter, my husband tried to decipher the hieroglyphics as best he could.

> Men need their wives close by whenever they're attempting to assemble anything.

He wasn't totally lost, though, because he had me. Men need their wives close by whenever they're attempting to assemble anything. Who else can answer those tough questions like, "Where's my hammer?" "What'd you do with my screwdriver?" and "Why can't I ever find my tools when I need them?"

After they've worked until the wee hours of the morning to complete the project, who else but a loving wife would have the nerve to point out those three screws and two nuts that are always left over? (No matter what the project, there are always three screws and two nuts left over. Assemble a bike, there are three screws and two nuts left over. Build a dollhouse, there are three screws and two nuts left over. Personally, I think it's some sort of sick packaging joke.)

In spite of the instructions and the leftover parts, my husband somehow had the swing set up and operational just before dawn broke over the horizon. It was beautiful. A monument to parental perseverance. As soon as the children woke up, we tricked them into going outside. They saw the swing set and were so excited, they stayed out there playing on it for hours.

Now, this story would have remained a warm, wonderful Christmas memory if it weren't for one little fact. That year we also bought our sons their own toolboxes, each complete with hammer, socket wrench, screwdriver and more.

While my husband and I were busy making a holiday fire out of all the empty boxes and wrapping paper, the boys had their own little project going. The swing set and tool set together proved to be too much of a temptation, and on one of our trips outside to check on them, we discovered that they had dismantled the entire thing! And they didn't even need the directions to do it.

All the pieces were lying in a pile in the middle of the sandbox, and the boys were standing ever so proudly next to them. It was one of those moments when you don't know whether to laugh, cry, applaud their mechanical skills or return the tool set to the store before they knock out a wall and add a rumpus room to the house.

We opted to laugh about it. Besides, Dad could put it back together again. By now, he was an expert at reading the directions.

"The directions!" my husband screamed, racing to the fireplace just in time to see them swallowed up in flames.

The kids are all grown up now, but Dad still works on it every weekend.

"Now let's see . . . that was insert A into B . . ."

Martha Bolton

Christmas waves a magic wand over this world, and behold, everything is softer and more beautiful.

Norman Vincent Peale

Holidays are happy days, and happy days are all too few; so celebrate them with people you love. I hope you'll recover in time to do them all again next year!

Mary Hollingsworth

Credits

CHAPTER ONE—HAPPILY EVER LAUGHTER

All material that originally appeared in *Daily Guideposts* and *Guideposts* magazine is reprinted with permission. Copyright © 1991, 1994, 1997, 2001 by Guideposts. All rights reserved.

Bigger, Margaret G. *Churchgoers' Chuckles*. Charlotte, NC: A. Borough Books, 2000.

Bonham, Tal D. *The Treasury of Clean Jokes*. Nashville, TN: Broadman & Holman, 1997.

Brunsting, Bernard. *The Ultimate Guide to Good Clean Humor*. Uhrichsville, OH: Barbour, 2000. Used by permission.

Taken from *God Uses Cracked Pots* by Patsy Clairmont, a Focus on the Family book published by Tyndale House Publishers. Copyright © 1999, Patsy Clairmont. All rights reserved. International copyright secured. Used by permission.

Cloninger, Claire and Karla Worley. *When the Glass Slipper Doesn't Fit and The Silver Spoon is in Someone Else's Mouth*. Birmingham, AL: New Hope, 2003.

Fadiman, Clifton. *The Faber Book of Anecdotes*. London: Faber, 1985.

"You're My Best Friend." Taken from *Chocolate Chili Pepper Love*. Copyright © 2000 by Becky Freeman. Published by Harvest House Publishers, Eugene, OR. www.harvesthousepublishers.com. Used by permission.

Larson, Bruce. *The One and Only You*. Dallas: Word, 1974.

"Husband for Sale." Reprinted from *Detours, Tow Trucks and Angels in Disguise* © 1996 by Carol Kent. Used by permission of NavPress, Colorado Springs, CO. All rights reserved.

Kraus, James. *Bloopers, Blunders, Quips, Jokes, and Quotes*. Wheaton, IL: Tyndale, 2005. Used by permission.

Taken from *The Art of Understanding Your Mate* by Cecil Osborne. Copyright © 1988 by Cecil Osborne. Used by permission of The Zondervan Corporation.

Stibbe, Mark and J. John. *A Bucket of Surprises*. Oxford, UK: Monarch, 2002.

———. *A Barrel of Fun*. Oxford, UK: Monarch, 2003.

Woods, Ralph L. *The Modern Handbook of Humor*. New York: McGraw-Hill, 1967.

CHAPTER TWO—FUNNY BONE FITNESS

All material that originally appeared in *Daily Guideposts* and *Guideposts* magazine is reprinted with permission. Copyright © 1998, 2002, 2005 by Guideposts. All rights reserved.

Bolton, Martha. *Didn't My Skin Used to Fit?* Grand Rapids, MI: Bethany House, a division of Baker Publishing Group, 2000.

"I Never Met a Cookie I Didn't Fall in Love With," reprinted from *Move Over Victoria—I Know the Real Secret*. Copyright © 2000 by Nancy Kennedy. Used by permission of WaterBrook Press, Colorado Springs, CO. All rights reserved.

Excerpted from *Normal Is Just a Setting On Your Dryer* by Patsy Clairmont, a Focus on the Family book published by Tyndale House Publishers. Copyright © 1993, Patsy Clairmont. All rights reserved. International copyright secured. Used by permission.

Copyright © 1999 by Marie Evans and Ann Shakeshaft. Reprinted from the book *Red Hot Mamas Do Menopause with Style* with permission of its publisher, Sourcebooks, Inc. (800-432-7444).

Taken from *Coffee Cup Friendship and Cheesecake Fun*. Copyright © 2001 by Becky Freeman. Published by Harvest House Publishers, Eugene, OR. www.harvesthousepublishers.com. Used by permission.

"Thin People Don't" originally published in *Feeding the Hungry Heart* (Bobbs-Merrill) and then in *McCall's*, this piece was written by Barbara

Florio Graham, award-winning author and writing teacher, whose Web site is www.SimonTeakettle.com.

Hollingsworth, Mary. "To Tell the Truth." Administered by Shady Oaks Studio, 1507 Shirley Way, Bedford, TX 76022. Used by permission.

John, Killy and Alie Stibbe. *Bursting at the Seams.* Oxford, UK: Monarch, 2004.

Kraus, James. *Bloopers, Blunders, Quips, Jokes, and Quotes.* Wheaton, IL: Tyndale, 2005. Used by permission.

Phillips, Bob. *The World's Greatest Collection of Clean Jokes.* Eugene, OR: Harvest House, 1998. Used by permission. www.harvesthousepublishers.com.

Phillips, Cathy Lee. *Aging, Ailments, and Attitudes.* Canton, GA: Patchwork Press, 2003. Used by permission. www.cathyleephillips.com.

Youngman, Henny. *The Encyclopedia of One Liners by Henny Youngman.* Katonah, NY: Ballymote, 1989.

CHAPTER THREE—ANIMAL ANTICS

All material that originally appeared in *Daily Guideposts* and *Guideposts* magazine is reprinted with permission. Copyright © 1983–2005 by Guideposts. All rights reserved.

Kraus, James. *Bloopers, Blunders, Quips, Jokes, and Quotes.* Wheaton, IL: Tyndale, 2005. Used by permission.

Stibbe, Mark and J. John. *A Bucket of Surprises.* Oxford, UK: Monarch, 2002.

Taken from *Extravagant Grace* by Patsy Clairmont, Barbara E. Johnson, Meberg, Marilyn, Luci Swindoll, Sheila Walsh, and Thelma Wells. Copyright © 2000 by Women of Faith, Inc. Used by permission of The Zondervan Corporation.

Richmond, Gary. *A View from the Zoo.* Nashville: W Publishing Group, 1987. More of Gary's stories can be found in *A New View from the Zoo*, published by DMJ Media Group.

CHAPTER FOUR—ON THE HIGHWAY TO HUMOR

All material that originally appeared in *Daily Guideposts* and *Guideposts* magazine is reprinted with permission. Copyright © 1991, 1994, 1997, 2001 by Guideposts. All rights reserved.

Beard, Zarette. "Camp Run-A-Mok." © 2007 Zarette Beard. Used by permission. All rights reserved. ZaretteBeard@yahoo.com.

Bonham, Tal D. *The Treasury of Clean Jokes*. Nashville, TN: Broadman & Holman, 1997.

Hogan, Gabe. "A Bitter Welcome." Used by permission. All rights reserved.

Harmon, Dan. *Book of Clean Jokes*. Uhrichsville, OH: Barbour, 2004. Used by permission.

Hollingsworth, Mary. "Head 'em Up, Move 'em Out!" Administered by Shady Oaks Studio, 1507 Shirley Way, Bedford, TX 76022. Used by permission. All rights reserved.

———. "Ten Ways to Know Your Family Vacation was a Success." Used by permission. All rights reserved.

———. "The Great Underwear Escapade." Used by permission. All rights reserved.

Humes, James C. *Podium Humor*. New York: Harper, 1975.

Kraus, James. *Bloopers, Blunders, Quips, Jokes, and Quotes*. Wheaton, IL: Tyndale, 2005. Used by permission.

Leeuwis, Martin. www.aviation-humor.com.

Peel, Kathy. *Stomach Virus and Other Forms of Family Bonding*. Nashville: W Publishing, a division of Thomas Nelson, Inc., 1993. All rights reserved.

Richards, Laura E. "Child's Play" from *The Golden Windows*. New York: Little, Brown, 1928.

CHAPTER FIVE—JEST PATRIOTIC

All material that originally appeared in *Daily Guideposts* and *Guideposts* magazine is reprinted with permission. Copyright © 1981–2006 by Guideposts. All rights reserved.

Bolton, Martha. *Honey, The Carpet Needs Weeding Again.* Ann Arbor, MI: Servant, 1993. Used by permission.

Bromley, Michael L. Taft anecdotes found on http://bromleyisms.stretching-it .com. Used by permission.

Cohen, Ben. "The Top 9 Pentagon Ice Cream Names." Found on www.topfive .com/top10lists.html. Courtesy of TopFive.com.

Graham, Vicki. "Carolyn to Tower." Used by permission.

Hollingsworth, Mary. "My Other Daddy." Administered by Shady Oaks Studio, 1507 Shirley Way, Bedford, TX 76022. Used by permission. All rights reserved.

Kraus, James. *Bloopers, Blunders, Quips, Jokes, and Quotes.* Wheaton, IL: Tyndale, 2005. Used by permission.

Leeuwis, Martin. "Forced Landing." www.aviation-humor.com.

Paxton, Bill. "To Honor a Veteran." All rights reserved.

Ward, William Arthur. "My Name Is America." All rights reserved. Used by permission.

CHAPTER SIX—LITTLE WONDERS

All material that originally appeared in *Daily Guideposts* and *Guideposts* magazine is reprinted with permission. Copyright © 1991, 1994, 1997, 2001 by Guideposts. All rights reserved.

Brunsting, Bernard. *Light Up Your Life with a Laugh.* © 1993. Used by permission.

Hafer, Todd and Jedd. *Snickers From the Front Pew.* Colorado Springs, CO: Cook Communications, 2000. All rights reserved.

Hogan, Rhonda. "And Take Us to Heaven." Used by permission of Creative Solutions, Arlington, TX 76016.

Hollingsworth, Mary. "A Logical Question." Administered by Shady Oaks Studio, 1507 Shirley Way, Bedford, TX 76022. Used by permission.

———. "You Know You're a Kid When." Administered by Shady Oaks Studio, 1507 Shirley Way, Bedford, TX 76022. Used by permission.

Myers, James. *A Treasury of Medical Humor*. South Bend, IN: And Books, 1993. Used by permission.

Phillips, Bob. *The World's Greatest Collection of Clean Jokes*. Eugene, OR: Harvest House, 1998. Used by permission. www.harvesthousepublishers.com

Stibbe, Mark and J. John. *A Box of Delights*. Oxford, UK: Monarch, 2001.

Streiker, Lowell D. *Nelson's Big Book of Laughter*. Nashville, TN: Thomas Nelson, 2000. Used by permission of Thomas Nelson, Inc.

Wolfe, Digby. "Here's to the Kids Who are Different." © 1982 Used by permission.

The World's Greatest Collection of Church Jokes. Uhrichsville, OH: Barbour, 2003. Used by permission.

CHAPTER SEVEN—CASH IN ON LAUGHTER

All material that originally appeared in *Daily Guideposts* and *Guideposts* magazine is reprinted with permission. Copyright © 1991, 1994, 1997, 2001 by Guideposts. All rights reserved

Ford, Joe Taylor. *The Executive Speechwriter Newsletter*. St. Johnsbury, VT: Words Ink, 1990.

Hollingsworth, Mary. Administered by Shady Oaks Studio, 1507 Shirley Way, Bedford, TX 76022. Used by permission. All rights reserved.

Kraus, James. *Bloopers, Blunders, Quips, Jokes, and Quotes*. Wheaton, IL: Tyndale, 2005. Used by permission.

Lyles, Cleon. *Wish I'd Said That*. Morrilton, AR: © 1970 by Cleon Lyles.

Myers, James. *A Treasury of Religious Humor*. South Bend, IN: And Books, 1993. Used by permission.

Offutt, Jason. "Dad, I Need a . . . What?" Used by permission. www.jasonoffutt.com.

Phillips, Bob. *Great Thoughts and Funny Sayings*. Wheaton, IL: Tyndale, 1993.

Wall, P. S. *My Love is Free . . . But the Rest of Me Don't Come Cheap.* Nashville: Rutledge Hill, 1997. Used by permission of author. Paula Wall is the author of the national best-selling novels *The Rock Orchard* and *The Wilde Women* (Atria).

Youngman, Henny. *The Best Little Book of One Liners.* Philadelphia: Running Press, 1992.

CHAPTER EIGHT—HOLIDAY HILARITY

All material that originally appeared in *Daily Guideposts* and *Guideposts* magazine is reprinted with permission. Copyright © 1998–2005 by Guideposts. All rights reserved.

Bolton, Martha. *If You Can't Stand the Smoke, Stay Out of My Kitchen.* Kansas City: Beacon Hill Press, 1990. Used by permission of author.

Eisenberg, Helen and Larry. *The Public Speaker's Handbook of Humor.* Grand Rapids, MI: Baker, 1972.

Hogan, Rhonda. Administered by Creative Solutions, 6205 Barcelona, Arlington, TX 76016. Used by permission. All rights reserved.

Hollingsworth, Mary. Administered by Shady Oaks Studio, 1507 Shirley Way, Bedford, TX 76022. Used by permission. All rights reserved.

Kraus, James. *Bloopers, Blunders, Quips, Jokes, and Quotes.* Wheaton, IL: Tyndale, 2005. Used by permission.

Palmer, Sharon Mason. "Toothless Grin." Used by permission. All rights reserved. For other stories by author, contact her at sharon-palmer@mindless.com.

Stibbe, Mark and J. John. *A Barrel of Fun.* Oxford, UK: Monarch, 2003.

Swindoll, Luci. *You Bring the Confetti.* Copyright © 1997 by Luci Swindoll. All rights reserved.

Tucker, Ginger. "Do You Know Bailey's Jesus?" Copyright Ginger Tucker 2006. From *Dancing On Daddy's Feet and Other Stories of God's Love,* written by Ginger Tucker and published by GKT Publishing, Amarillo, Texas. For ordering information visit www.gingertucker.com. Used by permission. All rights reserved.

A Note From the Editors

This original book was created by the Books and Inspirational Media Division of Guideposts, the world's leading inspirational publisher. Founded in 1945 by Dr. Norman Vincent Peale and Ruth Stafford Peale, Guideposts helps people from all walks of life achieve their maximum personal and spiritual potential. Guideposts is committed to communicating positive, faith-filled principles for people everywhere to use in successful daily living.

Our publications include award-winning magazines such as *Guideposts* and *Angels on Earth*, best-selling books, and outreach services that demonstrate what can happen when faith and positive thinking are applied in day-to-day life.

For more information, visit us at www.guideposts.com, call (800) 932-2145 or write Guideposts, PO Box 5815, Harlan, Iowa 51593.